JONATHAN FISK comes of age in W[...] mature Reformational theology, galvani[...] technosocial, consumeristic culture and also by his extensive experience in pastoral ministry. His reflections coalesce in a passionate new work that's hypercharged to motivate his readers to *do* something about a flaccid, passive, largely capitulated-to-culture Christianity that has rendered the message of Jesus indistinguishable from godless Humanitarianism's ethic of neighborly niceness. But, Fisk says, that's not the Gospel; it never was. Such a pathetic, this-world-is-all-there-is, message shrinks before American Liberalism as if Jesus were dead and His Gospel were weak. At the heart of Evangelical Christianity's surrender to today's dictum that "human morality is good enough" is a loss of confidence in the truth of God's Word and, significantly, the power of God's Word proclaimed and sacramented. Think, then, of *Without Flesh* as a clarion call to the Church to *be* the Church, to Christians to *be* fearless in their possession of Jesus' message of truth and hope. Christ is not dead. He is very much alive and very much in charge. It's time to live and speak in light of that reality, just as St. Paul in pagan Imperial Rome, just as Martin Luther in political Roman Catholicism. It's time to push back against the zeitgeist with the Spirit of Christ. Blending the reckless allegiance to Christ by the Church Fathers with the boldness of Luther and Hermann Sasse's prescience, Jonathan Fisk urges "old-fashioned faithful grit" because Christianity cannot die, because Jesus is not dead, because Christ is in fact the world's rightful King.

> John J. Bombaro, PhD, King's College, University of London
> Director of Theological Education for Eurasia, Rīga Luther
> Academy, Latvia

TO A CHURCH cowering in the corner, Pastor Fisk's *Without Flesh* bursts into the room with a dazzling light. It rallies us. It emboldens us. "Don't be afraid! 'This is My body! This is My blood!' These words of Jesus still stand true!" The Church finds her life in hearing these words and eating this flesh. This book gives boldness and courage by fixing our ears and our lips on the Word made flesh for us.

> Bryan Wolfmueller, author of *A Martyr's Faith in a Faithless World*
> pastor of St. Paul Lutheran Church and Jesus Deaf Lutheran
> Church, Austin, Texas

WHY HAD SO MANY in Corinth become weak and ill? For the same reason faith dies in those who cling to a faddish, false, and crossless "Christianity" today. Rev. Jonathan Fisk's *Without Flesh* is a surgical exploration of the cancer afflicting much of nominal Christianity today: doubt in, disuse of, and lack of trust in the words of Christ that established the Lord's Supper and in the life-giving forgiveness and medicine of immortality He gives according to His promise. Poignant and pithy, bluntly honest and boldly faithful, *Without Flesh* will point readers to the Word made flesh, Christ Himself, who creates, nurtures, and resurrects faith unto life everlasting.

> Rev. Paul Cain, editor of *Lutheran Book Review*
> senior pastor of Immanuel Lutheran Church, Sheridan, Wyoming

AMID PROTESTANT and Gnostic denials of the absolute validity of the divine Word and the miracle of Jesus' Holy Supper, Pastor Fisk cautions us to examine the easily misused call to "change or die." He marshals the Rock of Horeb (1 Corinthians 10), the three who bear witness (water, blood, and Spirit), Jesus' great "I am" statements, and more, trumpeting the call to "change *back*" to the present and enduring coming in the flesh that Jesus does in the Sacrament.

> Rev. Dr. Kenneth Wieting, retired LCMS pastor
> author of *The Blessings of Weekly Communion* and
> *Lutheranism 101: The Lord's Supper*

WITHOUT FLESH

Why the Church Is Dying Even Though Jesus Is Still Alive

WITH FLE

CONCORDIA PUBLISHING HOUSE · SAINT LOUIS

OUTSH

WHY

THE CHURCH

IS DYING

EVEN THOUGH

JESUS IS

STILL ALIVE

JONATHAN FISK

Dedication

For good reason.
And, as always, for you.

Published by Concordia Publishing House
3558 S. Jefferson Avenue, St. Louis, MO 63118-3968
1-800-325-3040 • cph.org

1   2   3   4   5   6   7   8   9   10   29   28   27   26   25   24   23   22   21   20

Contents

Acknowledgments

THANK GOD for Hermann Sasse, and thank God also for Rev. Matthew Harrison for the work he and others have undertaken to translate and make available Dr. Sasse for those of us who cannot read German. I am eternally indebted.

Unless otherwise noted, all Sasse quotations are taken from the essay "Church and Lord's Supper," published originally in 1938, now available in the compendium *The Lonely Way*, vol. 1, pp. 369ff.

Except where otherwise indicated, Bible quotations are taken from the English Standard Version. Cited verses are noted, but the entire verse is not always quoted. At times, the quotation only includes a portion of a verse or sentence, but in all cases I end the quotation with a period for the sake of clarity.

only hunger
brings people
to church

Prologue

IN 1939, the Nazis were marching through the streets on their way to "liberate" France. Since 1935, people of Hebraic descent had been ghettoed, but the true Holocaust was not yet begun. Even so, the Christian chance to respond was already far past. The 1934 Barmen Declaration, signed by many Christian pastors as a rejection of the Nazi control of the churches, had done nothing to slow infiltration of Nazi ideology and power in both congregations and culture. Now the pulpits were preached in by double agents. Now the Gospel was outlawed as an offense to Arian morality. Now Dr. Hermann Sasse, ever the stalwart and brave confessor, first among his colleagues to speak out against the Fascist propagandas when they originally appeared, decided to write an open letter to the world about the grave situation they faced.

His topic of choice? The Lord's Supper.

With Christianity in shambles, with the buildings entirely lost to the activities of an alien and hostile power, with the bad people in control and the good people too terrified to speak, Sasse, with pristine, cosmic insight, like the prophets of old, ignored the frills and distractions of immediacy and took an ax to the root.

To understand why is, in part, the purpose of this book. For while it may seem on the surface that we live in times a million ideas removed from the depths of Nazi Germany, appearances can be deceiving. Humanity has not changed. Our doubtfulness has not changed. Our tendency toward hysteria has not changed.

But Sasse's reasoning will have to work its own magic. To see with his precision, you will need to make room for his arguments. To perceive where present and past combine, you will need to sit for a while with the eternal. This begins not at the Lord's Supper itself but at its root. At the Church's root. At Christianity's root. With Jesus Christ Himself.

The Crisis of Crosslessness

What is wrong with our church?
What is wrong with each one of us
and our faith if such disintegration
of our church was possible?

Hermann Sasse

Quid incertitudine imserius? [What
is more wretched than uncertainty?]

Martin Luther

Jesus Christ is the same yesterday
and today and forever.

Anonymous

Don't Change

UPHEAVAL is all around us. A messy dark age of misinformation, distraction, and willfulness dominates us. Civilization trembles, besieged by gusts and surges. Impregnable institutions are collapsing while, by wit, will, and luck, power brokers ride the waves at a mad pace. In the midst of all this, for anything still trying to call itself a "church," it is a terrifying time to be in business, much less to actively sail against the tide.

But is any of it truly new? Or do we merely believe it to be so? To be sure, compared with memories of those greener pastures of only a few decades ago, pews are emptier, congregation budgets are dwindled, and church doors are closing. There's no question about that. It all looks authentically bleak.

Yet what we must consider is what precisely the bleakness **means**.

Have the times really changed? Is the Church actually dying? Are we truly in danger of being subsumed beneath a new, ominous culture of evil? Or is the only real difference a matter of our perspective? Is the only real change the fact that we have convinced ourselves that times have changed?

Change is often spoken of as if it is its own kind of religion. Some fear it and avoid it at all costs. Others trust it implicitly, regardless of the results. Whichever side of the coin you are on, both parties are too quick to grant "change" near godlike powers. If Christianity is a **holy spirituality** founded to outlast even the end of the world, aren't we overreacting a bit? Twitter gets invented, and boom! The almighty dominion of the Lord of lords is suddenly in question?

What?

It's kind of like watching sailors on a boat far from shore. They notice signs of a storm approaching. But rather than batten down the hatches, they decide that now would be a good time to renovate the whole boat from the hull up. "Anchors? Who needs anchors? Hey you! Get over here and slice up that sail. It's a bit medieval, don't you think?"

"And ropes? Ropes are sexist. Toss those overboard, quick, before someone sees them. Hop to it, ye scurvy dogs! We need to get moving now! We need to change what we're doing . . . or die!"

But does the approaching storm warrant this? Will any change help, or would some changes be useful while others only make the situation worse? Are these questions even being asked?

In American Christianity, this "change or die" refrain has become its own form of creed. Within little more than a generation or two, it has accompanied the erosion of Christianity's presence in society. In a brief time, nearly two millennia of conviction that historic Christianity is the last bastion of humanity's hope have been replaced. Instead, there sits the new assumption that we are about to face such a perfect storm of change that unless the Church finds a way to join its maddening pace, Christianity is fully and rightly doomed.

the new creed is "change or die"

Down to a skeleton crew, with no rudder or mast to be seen, and the few remaining officers frantically drilling holes in the hull while cackling, "The answer! At last! The answer!" one has to wonder how long until they set to work bailing water into the boat. The shoals loom deadly close. Leviathan waits in the depths with open maw.

Yes. It looks *damned* bleak. And I'm not cursing. There is something terribly diabolical at work.

But allow me to suggest that even such impending doom is not nearly so bad as it might seem, especially when you've got Christianity on your side. And all the lukewarm spiritual attention, all the shrinking congregations, all the collapsing moralities and apostatizing children are *not* unique.

Allow me to insist that our times are *nothing new*.

For the vast bulk of history, times like our own have been the tragic consistency. There is only one new wind that is blowing among us, and that is the wind of believing that we're so very different from everything that came before.

Empires collapsing? What of it?

The love of many is growing cold? You are surprised by this?

People who grew up in church aren't going anymore? Welcome to Sadland. Welcome to Normalsville.

The churches of our age have forgotten that they are not here to build a kingdom in the present but to herald the impending better one? Been there, done that too. Tickets to the Reformation, anyone?

The only truly new idea of our age is the suggestion that our age is new.

And even this isn't really that new of an idea. But it does remain the one idea that everyone believes, the granted "truth" that none of us are willing to question.

our times are nothing new

I don't care. I think the idea that times have changed is a stupid idea.

Take a deep breath and dwell on that. Let it be the faintest hint of a possibility. Pause and consider that maybe the only real problem we face is believing we face something new.

Maybe relevance, technology, and strategy are human realities that make precisely zero spiritual impact in Jesus' Church.

Maybe reactionary fearmongering and growth-minded fad peddling might not be the solution. Maybe they're the problem.

Certainly only a fool would board a ship whose crew throws all the food overboard at the first sign of a storm.

Only the same kind of fool would join a religion filled with adherents willing to jettison their most cherished beliefs at the first sign of people not believing them.

Only a narcissist would join a movement more concerned with getting him to join them than with moving him in their direction.

Only mania explains self-proclaimed followers of Jesus believing that they can convert people to His Spirit by *hiding* Jesus, by minimizing both His words and His most public works from all polite conversations.

Are today's Christians really so arrogant as to believe that the way to save Christianity is to cease clinging to it? Are today's Christians truly so blind as to willfully forget that the only real purpose of Christianity is to preach the radical message of trust in the body of a single man, and Him dead, hanging nailed to a cross? Do today's Christians actually think that our churches will long survive by willfully forgetting that the one thing universally guaranteed by Him to never pass away is His Word?

Jesus sends Christians into the world with the insistence that they are sheep among wolves. He did not give us a product to market or an ideology to debate. He gave a truth to be believed. He also told us that the world would hate that truth. Whether we are in the midst of the most bountiful new-Pentecost harvest the world has ever seen, or in the midst of a drought so bone-deep and out of season that even the tares are asking where the water might be, what is needed is not the doubt-riddled lunacy that we must "*change or die.*" What is needed is the old-fashioned faithful grit that believes that no matter what we see, Christianity will never die.

Because Christianity **cannot** die.

Because **Jesus is not dead**.

Take courage.

Have some moxie.

Grab a glass of tenacity with me.

Stop and *listen*.

Stop and *remember*.

Patience, grasshopper.

Zeal without knowledge is fire without light.

have some moxie: Christianity cannot die

There is a gut-deep, mind-transfiguring, change-invincible **faith** given in Jesus Christ "so that you may believe" (John 20:31) that no matter how bad it looks, the Church of Jesus Christ is not going anywhere.

Except *forever*.

Because **Jesus is alive**.

Jesus is not only a man of our past but the Lord of our present and our future. He submitted to death, not to get bound by it but in order to rip out its sting by the root. He rose again, not to abandon us but to bind Himself to us eternally. He ascended to the Father, not to leave us as orphans but to compel the first twelve men He left behind to "more than [conquer]" (Romans 8:37) the world.

Not by any means necessary.

Not as man saw fit.

But with an extreme, specific vision.

With an invested, marvelous, *particular* mission.

Authorized to wield a single, scandalous, peculiar, highly unbelievable, certifiably impossible, yet everlastingly eternal *promise*.

Not a guess.

Not a gimmick.

Not a gamble.

A plan.

"*Do this*," He said.

The Problem of Not Doing

Evangelical theology's burning wound . . . is that skepticism which no longer believes the Scriptures to be the Word of God.

Hermann Sasse

For the sake of my person and life I will humble myself before anyone and beg grace and favor from a child insofar as these people are not hostile to the Gospel. For I know that if it is strictly judged, my life earns nothing but the abyss of hell. But for the sake of my office and doctrine, and even of my life to the extent that it comes to these, let no one—particularly tyrants and persecutors of the Gospel—expect any patience or humility from me.

Martin Luther

All mankind are liars.

King David

Too Impatient to Hear

If the bugle gives an indistinct
sound, who will get ready for battle?
(1 Corinthians 14:8)

THERE HAVE been few religious events in history like the total retreat of Christianity from the front lines of Western culture. A brief visit to the church buildings on countless street corners reveals the stupendous reality that the majority of them are in danger of closing their doors at any minute. This is in spite of a century of best efforts to grow these churches at any cost and by any means. Despite these attempts, despite million-dollar industries devoted to Sunday Schools, youth groups, small groups, evangelism training, and more, once-core elements of Christianity are now all but unknown to professing Christians—children and adults alike.

Radically divided, there is little that remains to unite us short of the desperation driving us to turn these effects around. For all of our divisions, this is our unifying doctrine: a manic search driven by invincible faith that a silver bullet can be found that will return us to the glory days of better numbers and cultural relevance.

This is why we buy programs and scour books. We are hunting for some insight, some trend, some trick that will slip just enough people back into the pews . . . er . . . *cushioned chairs* to steer our ship back toward some "better day."

This is not how the first Christians stepped before the world. Unlike our fading postmodern echo, the first Christians were not in search of anything. They were convinced that they had already *found* it. They had a message. It made them *fearless*. And it was the fearlessness of their conviction that made them so compelling everywhere they went. The message was so truly charismatic, so life altering, that it only ever inspired one of two reactions: love or hate. There was no lukewarm. There was no middle ground. There was not peace but a sword dividing families, breaking up cultures, and turning the entire world upside down.

The Book of Acts, with marvelous detail, recounts not only the maddening pace at which this message spread through the first-century world but also the dynamic consistency of the message itself. Certainly, the gift of tongues gave the people a leg up on translation for a time, but the fact

what they found made them fearless

remained that no matter what tongue the message was spoken in, no ink needed to be spilled on figuring out *what* to say. As Acts details it, every time anyone opens his mouth in a moment of witness, regardless of context or culture or expected style, he repeats one, permanent refrain: "There was this particular, local dead guy, and He has refused to stay dead."

The first day it was spoken, thousands believed. But it is a sign of our modern, weak-kneed covetousness that we think the numbers are the thing that mattered. We forget that as stunning as all those first Baptisms certainly were, a far greater number than that went home *unbelieving* that same day. On that Pentecost day in Jerusalem, after the apostles preached with glowing heads, more people heard and *did not* believe than turned and repented. Afterward, day by day, more believers were added to their number, but this was *never* a majority of those who heard.

Yet this did not once convince them to change the message. They clung firmly to the same story, insisted on the same proclamation, and emphasized the infallible nature of the task they had been given. They did all this in spite of the fact that as more people believed, the worse the situation became for those who were the most public believers. Far from chartering private cruise liners and traveling the world in style, the preachers were promptly jailed. People were beaten. They were driven into hiding. They were murdered on account of their message by having rocks thrown at their faces over and over again.

Making matters even less exciting was the reality that wherever the story of Jesus' resurrection spread, the people who believed it were not the wise, the successful, and the royal. Those types all diligently stayed away. On Mars Hill, where the scholars lounged, they laughed at St. Paul.

Christianity was a religion that made its mark by converting the weak, the impoverished, and the unimpressive. These people did not become powerful, rich, or impending by their conversion. They became *fearless*. They were not fearless because their mission always succeeded, nor because their personal lives became suddenly marked by a string of divinely inspired victorious moments. As we would define *success* today, the early churches were total failures. They never won over the culture. They never dominated the market, and the vast majority of their leaders wound up dead before their time. Instead of detouring them, instead of turning them away, this is what inspired them. This is why they were fearless. This is how they demonstrated their courage.

They did not need to see in order to believe. Rather, they believed what they had heard, and this became in them the supernatural ability to see beyond the merely human possibilities of their present, evil age.

Now here we are, some two millennia later, arrogantly believing that we live in exceptional times. It is in *fear* of our present evil age we hear our churches preach, "We must change or die." It is the overt trust in what is seen that has stolen from us the power to convert.

The Threat

They were sawn in two. (Hebrews 11:37)

IMAGINE a moment when you and I sit down for coffee at a local shop. I reach into my satchel and pull out a folder filled with documents. These documents present study after study done by reputable, world-class companies. These studies demonstrate beyond any reasonable doubt that preaching the texts of the Bible in today's market conditions guarantees the gradual emptying of the pews of your local church. One hundred percent. There is no debate. The evidence is incontrovertible. Jesus' actual words not only will not grow your church—they will shrink it. Quickly. Keep preaching the Bible's actual text, and within half a decade, you will be in financial straits. You will be stretching your last few volunteers even further. You won't just be wondering where next year's budget will come from; you will be selling the building. You will no longer be struggling to pay a part-time pastor; you will be defaulting on your bills and loans.

It's hypothetical, of course. I don't have this kind of proof. But I want you to consider it a possibility for the sake of this question: *If* it were shown to be true, **what would you do?** Would you want the Scriptures preached anyway? It means you will close. It means your pastor will have to work part time and serve three other churches. It means your kids might not get married at the same altar as you. Do you still want to stand firm?

Now, let's up the ante.

What if I pulled out another folder? In this folder, I show you further clear proof that this same tactic will not only empty your pews over the next twenty years, but it will also put you on your government's watch lists. It shows that clinging to the Bible's words will not only put your local congregation in danger, but it will also threaten your mortgage. Your children's ability to attain an education. Your spouse's ability to receive health care.

What if I showed you proof that continuing to attend your church's services could reasonably get you killed?

Would you still go?

Would you still insist that the Scriptures be preached? Clearly? Irrevocably?

Isn't it amazing that this is a question that can even give us pause as we consider it?

The Death of Conviction

> Am I now seeking the approval of man, or of God? (Galatians 1:10)

THE ANCIENT Church saw martyrdom as an honor. Today, we cower in corners, bickering over the color of the carpet. The Ancient Church conquered the world by dying at its hands. Today, we are crushed in an overwhelming retreat of trying to fit in.

The Ancient Church did not have better marketing. They did not have better tactics. They did not have better funding. They simply *believed* that they were on a ship that *could not* sink. They carried a message that *could not* be silenced. They were the Body of a Christ who *could not* die.

Christianity, they believed, was unable to pass away, even though heaven and earth themselves passed away. Even while to the whole world it appeared that they were sinking, even if before the world they were publicly being murdered, the *words* of Jesus were ultimate bulwarks to them. He spoke unassailable truth.

Today, our knees quake at the first thought of a dip in our numbers. We chase efficiency as if it were a god. We pander after technology as if it were a spiritual gift. We whimper and cajole about passion, wondering why no one wants to listen to us. Every year the Body is weaker. Every year, individual Christians are more timid. Every year, our hope is more atrophied. We ignore these failed results of all our changes and throw on still more spit and polish, more elbow grease, and more sacramentally entrepreneurial enthusiasm for modern measures.

It has been well over a century now that salesmen hawking "change" for the churches have barked their now-tired pitches. The same song and dance repeated ad nauseam has not slowed us from buying what they're selling. But the tragic diagnosis is that all our decades upon decades of changing like gangbusters has done nothing to stop the soul from being sucked right out of visible Western Christianity. In fact, far from improving our situation, changing even the outer forms of Christianity has had the opposite effect.

That today we are still hearing calls for "change" shouted with such passion ought to boggle our minds. How many times does a village return to a poisoned well before they decide to stop drinking? How many times may a snake oil salesman visit the same town before the people finally remember his face and decide to run him off?

"Change" has been enacted for generations now, constantly boasting of the promise to make things better for the churches. But the results have been catastrophic. Today's renewed promises that we can halt our cultural slide into chaos by yet again reinventing a Christianity more relevant to the culture are the brandishing of a wild-eyed unawareness for just how desperately our many previous attempts have failed.

No one out there is listening to us anymore. We're talking in an echo chamber. Which is getting smaller. And smaller.

I believe that the reason people are not listening is because the pursuit of relevance is the admission of irrelevance. A religion that hungers for change only proves that it has already changed too much to survive. The belief that you need a better style with which to sell your substance is a confession that you have no substance at all.

the words of Jesus are bulwarks of truth

People are not listening to us because we have nothing to actually say. All that we market and all that we strategize and all that we mimic amounts to gibberish babbled on the wind.

Good old-fashioned pragmatism ought to give us pause in any case. Once a world religion has spent a century and billions of dollars doing anything, only to simultaneously embark on the most precipitous decline in its two-thousand-year history, it's probably time to stop tinkering with the formula and take another look at the original recipe.

It is precisely the words of Jesus that are *the thing* that ancient Christianity fearlessly sought to convert unbelievers *into*. Even should the earth have opened up and swallowed them into the sea, they would have merely continued to repeat the everlasting things of God with their mouths. They died willingly, merrily even, because they were convicted that such everlasting things made them into everlasting people. The last thing they would have ever conceived of doing would have been changing in order to convince more people to join them. Such a tactic would have been the very defeat of its own purpose.

Missing Parts

> Whoever speaks, as one who speaks oracles of God . . . . (1 Peter 4:11)

WHEN A MAN is addicted to drugs, finding more drugs always seems a very fine idea. If he knows anything at all, he knows that he needs a fix to his problem. But what he does not believe is that it is his fixes that are slowly killing him. What he will not believe is that the fixes are the cause of the problem.

If your computer stops working, downloading more apps for it will not improve your situation. If the source of the problem is viruses embedded in the apps, then adding more apps may just make it worse. It doesn't matter what software you install if the problem is with your hardware. If you want to diagnose the problem, what you really need to do is start paring back all the things you've customized since you bought it. You need to slowly remove everything that wasn't part of the original working specs.

Doing this, you might find that the problem was caused by something you've added. Then again, once you've gotten all the way back down to the core design, you might also discover that a key component has gone missing. Whether that missing piece is hardware or software doesn't matter. What matters is that your computer will never work again unless you go in and put that missing piece back.

you must put the missing piece back

For the Church in any age to make such a diligent search is a good idea. This always means going back to the words of Jesus.

Unfortunately, these days, that is easier said than done.

Where Might Jesus Be?

If we do not take what Scripture says concerning the presence of Christ with complete seriousness, then we have a wrong understanding of Christ. Then we also have a wrong understanding of his church. Then we have a mental construct of Christ in place of the real Christ, and in place of the real church, in which Jesus Christ is really present according to both his divinity *and* his humanity, we have a dream church, a mere community of spirits in which Christ is only spiritually present just as he was prior to his incarnation.

Hermann Sasse

Where Christ is, there is the Church.

Ignatius of Antioch

In the place that He will choose, to make His name dwell there, you shall eat the tithe of your grain, of your wine.

Moses, Prince of Egypt

Showdown at the *Ecclesia* Corral

Did God actually say . . . ? (Genesis 3:1)

IT WAS AN epic day in Churchtown. This was long before the huckster pulpits came through, selling their snake-oiled silver bullets to fix whatever ails your lagging congregation. This was the age of big tents and fresh promises, of grandiose dreams and the premonition of a dynamic battle about to be either won or lost.

Indeed, a host of bandits were in the hills, growing more brave by the year, ever coming closer to town while waving their weapons in the air. Though the people of Churchtown slept well at night, small victories were being won over little farms on the outskirts day by day.

The fight was all about the meaning of "meaning." It did not take place on little prairies or anywhere near real tumbleweeds. The fight was fought in the dry and dusty towers of academia. Those ivory halls were the rugged hills that the good people of Churchtown did not always tread, and it was there that a few wizened spiritual outlaws managed to take up strongholds from which to launch their long and slow assault.

The great insight to which these men of ambition had come, the single path by which they believed they could eventually take over Churchtown and more, was the realization that human beings, when we speak with one another, are capable of being misunderstood. While on the surface this may not seem like a stunning insight, this was indeed their own silver bullet, which, when carefully and studiously relied upon, would win them the battle.

The argument itself goes something like this:

"What I say" and "what you hear" are not always the same thing, and this is proven by misunderstandings that arise between us. But this means that there must be something more at work in our conversations than the mere "words." As it turns out, the "words" in our talk are not entirely fixed things. ***The words are not the meaning***. The words are the sounds or inkblots we use to represent the meaning. But these inkblots and sounds are semifluid, capable of doing more than one thing at once.

This is where confusion can enter in. I say "dog," and I imagine my dog, a brown beagle named Hopper. But you hear "dog," and you imagine your neighbor's dog, a one-eyed yippy dachshund that thinks it is a Doberman.

See? Confusion.

This is the root of the entire argument. It is without question a **truth**. It is an unhappy accident of biblical history that this little incident with a tower at a place called Babel led to the utter imperfection of all human language. It is the truth that man's mouth is now broken, but it hardly undoes in itself the power of words to have any real meaning at all. More than this, it is only one side to the coin of the history of salvation in Jesus Christ, the other side of which is the day of Pentecost, on which God powerfully demonstrated that however limited we might be by our languages, He reserves the prerogative to speak right through the midst of them without being misunderstood— even a word.

Yet to these Wild West wizards held up in their ivory caves, Babel is but a myth meant to explain human migration, and Pentecost is a tall tale meant to centralize the medieval Roman governments. Freed from such niceties as the belief in the resurrection of Jesus, they had the stunning insight that **because** words are semifluid and not the equivalent of their own meaning, **therefore** meaning is but a figment of our imagination, a self-contained dream that, outside of each of our own individual heads, never really exists at all.

to these Wild West wizards, Babel is but a myth

Now, none of these cowboys of questioning ever willingly stepped in front of a bus to demonstrate the nonphysical existence of reality, nor did they cease from writing multivolume tomes in order to incontrovertibly prove their position that words have no meaning. Rather, with an endless stream of imperfect grunts and howls penciled into chicken scratch, they together exposed among themselves the nonexistence of knowledge itself. Feeling very smug and secure about this marvelous accomplishment, like finely monocled mobsters of thought, they began to circle the outskirts of Churchtown with their thoughtless thinking.

How this happened is a decades-long travesty of cultural decline. But **that** it happened is the more important point for our purpose. Whether we like their arguments or not, there is not one of us who has not heard it said, "Judge not, lest ye judge," much less the vaunted and pristine secular equivalent, "That is just your interpretation." These are the silver bullets of the materialistic marauders still at work among us.

So it came to pass that a day arose in Churchtown when the people looked out at their streets and found them emptier than they remembered them being. The few brave men who were willing to brave the barren streets soon found themselves ridden down by pillaging mobs of horsemen, white lab coats flickering in the wind behind them. Any who dared to stand up to them soon found that their trigger fingers were fast and sure. A horde of plausible arguments quickly alit against them in cacophony and rage, the smoky onslaught of assertion and claim.

"Understanding!" "Limitations!" "Nuances!"

"Change!"

The change that had taken place is that over the course of a century, the secular "discovery" that words can be confused had resulted in a church of Jesus Christ in which even Jesus Christ was not capable of speaking the unadulterated truth. He may have once been renowned as the Heavenly Ranger, a lone gunman untouched by the wild array of ages. But there is a new sheriff these days in Churchtown, and just like every Western you ever saw, he's not the land baron who's really in charge. He's the incompetent stooge with a badge who's too proud to notice that he's been played.

The Sheriff of Nothing New

> He has scattered the proud in the
> thoughts of their hearts. (Luke 1:51)

THE FIRST new sheriff believed himself a good man. He never intended for anything to go wrong. He was merely a student of truth. He had to be honest! Of course, all the townspeople believed that there had once been a Heavenly Ranger who had ridden into town long ago and saved all the people from the monsters who lived in the hills. But these were stories told to children to encourage them to be good.

No doubt there had once been some historic event that truly had happened. Some simple man, much like himself, had stood up to a coyote, or perhaps a wolf, maybe even saved a child or a damsel, and earned for himself the goodwill of the good people. But whoever He had been, the stories about Him had grown out of proportion of all that is reasonable. That bit about how He'd only ridden away to another town because He also intended to return one day and take up residence as mayor? Such things were plain superstition.

But now, things were different. There might have been a time when mere memories of this Ranger could keep the people going. When the only threats were coyotes and bad crops, a good story was well and good. But today, things were different. Here, they faced real bandits. Now, it was time to change—or die.

It was not easy for the sheriff to stand before the people, hat in hand, and explain to them how all their hopes were but a mere myth, and how it was now time to learn what that historical Ranger would have really wanted from them. It was a near Herculean task of courage to face down all their sad faces and tell them the truth that they didn't want to hear. It took a real master, a real hero, to explain to them how this was not a tragedy but an opportunity. This was not reason to despair. This was an opportunity for even greater things.

"This is no reason to fear," the sheriff said, making a fist in the air and holding it firm as he spoke. "No doubt, this was the Heavenly Ranger's *real* plan all along. He wanted you to learn how to stand up for yourself! That was why He stood up to that threat so long ago and then left. He knew that if He stayed, He would have disappointed us, but He didn't want us to ever disappoint ourselves. He wanted the memory of His one great moment to *inspire* us to make such moments of our own. Far from needing to be here to help us, He doesn't even need to have been real. All that really matters is the idea of Him. *That* is enough to help us help ourselves!"

The grit and steely glint in the sheriff's eye must have made his mother proud. But though he extolled and while he exhorted, it was nonetheless a sad and evident fact that from that day on, whenever the raiders came a-raiding, even fewer people than before seemed willing to stand up and fight back. He would shout, "For the Heavenly Ranger's memory!" working with all that was in him to make the memory of the story relevant as he ran out into the street. But in the end, he was only mown down himself in a tirade of time and plausible *pistolas*.

The sheriff who followed Him never had a chance. "We must change or die" was all that he could remember the former sheriff saying clearly. That much at least sounded smart. So, he repeated it, as did the man after him. But the more it was repeated, the more that posse of black-hatted skeptics took no notice of the deputies as they moseyed down the walks. The badged men would run up to them, shake their sidearm and shout about how they'd better take notice. But it was as if they didn't exist at all now, as if they were ghosts of the past.

"This is proof! They're ignoring us. We must change or die!"

And the people scatter.

And the streets stand empty in Churchtown.

And the words of the Heavenly Ranger can hardly be found.

The most amazing thing of all is that He's still standing right there in the street. The Heavenly Ranger is not gone but smack in the middle of everything. Not His memory. Not His story. **Him**.

The only thing that has changed is that we no longer believe it. One of the most dominant assumptions of modern Christianity is that Jesus has gone missing. He Supermanned it up to heaven and never looked back. If you want a piece of His Spirit now, well, that's up to you. You'd better start looking. You'd better start hoping. Because the last thing that anyone believes is that He is easy to find.

that much at least sounded smart

You believe this, and I can prove it to you. It's as simple as honestly answering this question off the cuff: *Isn't the ascension of Jesus the greatest news you ever heard?*

Because I know that your gut-response answer is no, I can comfortably tell you that a part of you still thinks you need to search for Jesus, or for the Holy Spirit, or for God. A major reason I wrote this book is to convince you that putting an end to such madness is not only possible but the very thing necessary if we're ever going to take our town back.

A Radical Idea

Behold, I am with you. (Matthew 28:20)

IF YOU'RE at all honest with yourself, you will admit that the ascension of Jesus Christ has always struck you as somewhat confusing. Because you are likely pious in your thinking, you are not in the habit of openly questioning public and historic actions of our Lord. But if pressed, you know that deep down, the ascension has always felt like one of the weirdest parts of Christianity.

It's okay. No one is watching. You can admit it. I won't tell.

I know it's what I've always thought. I mean, imagine how much better things would be for our churches if Jesus had stuck around. Think how much more effective all our mission efforts would be if the resurrected King were just sitting there on a throne over in Jerusalem, right where everyone could see Him. He'd be orchestrating His reign with faxes, emails, and press releases, along with a weekly hour-long broadcast to update all of us on how Christianity is going. With His power and authority, He'd put a stop to the tensions in world politics, and He could use His miracles to both heal the masses and silence skeptics. There'd never again be a church split or theological debate. A simple word from His mouth would answer all questions.

But instead the guy flies away to (literally!) God knows where. What is He thinking?

The answer to that question is even crazier than the question. But it also makes amazingly perfect sense. When Jesus ascended into heaven, *He never left*.

How can that be? Because the ascension of Jesus was not the moment when He took His human body out of the universe and to wherever God the Father's body is. God the Father doesn't have a body. No head, no heart, no right hand. God the Father, in His divinity, has the power to be in more than one place and in all places, all at once, and the ascension is the moment when Jesus, as a man, took up that same power for Himself.

the right hand of God is not a place but a power

This is what we used to call the *omnipresence* of God, and most Christians don't have any problem with Jesus' omnipresence when we talk about things like how He hears all our prayers, even as they are prayed all around the world, at all times and in all places. We believe that He not only hears but also answers. We believe that His eye is on the sparrow and that He is looking out for our good while also deftly wielding history toward a rapturous end. But for some reason, we don't see the connection between this miraculous ability and His ascension.

This is likely because we tend to think of the right hand of God as a *place*. We think of it as *somewhere* that someone might go. But this is all wrong. The definition of a place is that it is a location. It is *stuff* in *space*. But God the Father is not stuff, and He doesn't need space. He is beyond space, and time, and all the rest of creation. In this way, the right hand of God is *not a place* but a *power*. The "unapproachable light" of His dwelling that Paul mentions in 1 Timothy 6:16 is not somewhere that someone can go. It is the inability of anyone or anything to ever go there because it is to be God Himself.

Jesus is everywhere

But that is where Jesus went! That is what Jesus did. He didn't take His body to another place. He took His body into the ability to be in all places and no place all at once. By virtue of His Godness, He changed the capacity of His human body so that it no longer needed to be *local*. He no longer needs to be located in order to be somewhere. Without being located at all, He can now also be *everywhere*. He can "fill all things," as Paul says in Ephesians 4:10.

But here is the challenge with omnipresence. Since Jesus is everywhere, then that means that Jesus is everywhere. He is not just there in the "God things" and "Jesus sightings," those moments when everything turns out the way we hoped it would. The omnipresence of Jesus means that it is also a God thing every time something horrible happens. It is also a Jesus sighting every time things turn out in ways we didn't like or were not expecting. Jesus is there in far-off countries where the children don't have clean water. Jesus is there when a baby is born without a hand, or with a failing heart. Jesus is there when your mother gets cancer and dies.

Those are all God sightings too. They're just not the kind of God we want to believe in.

If Everyone Is Special, Then No One Is

I form light and create darkness;
I make well-being and create calamity.
(Isaiah 45:7)

WHEN WE SAY, *"If you have lemons, you make lemonade,"* we might be trying hard to make the best out of a bad situation. But sometimes it is better to simply admit that a bad situation is bad. There are times in life when there is no sugar to be found, or when all the sugar we've poured on the lemons turns out to be the cause of our diabetes. No matter how hard we pretend with blind hopefulness, reality always catches up.

No one at your funeral is going to say that your dead body is a God sighting. No one even thought that about Jesus' dead body, and yet that would have been profoundly true! Instead, at your funeral, those who love you will pay a great deal of money for flowers and a shiny casket and makeup in order to make it look like you're not really dead, even while they bury your carcass in order to keep it from stinking up the house.

They will hope that all of it will make it hurt less. It won't work. They'll mourn. They'll feel frustration and pain. They'll wonder, "Why?" And the God of omnipresence, the Jesus of omnipresence, won't be much comfort to them. Because He won't answer. He'll sit up there in heaven; He'll sit nowhere and everywhere and just watch. You can search behind the clouds or you can ask questions of the sky, but you won't get an answer. You'll only stand face-to-face with the wrath of the moment, the bare sinfulness of the world.

Trying to find Jesus in everything ultimately means that you cannot find Jesus anywhere. There are silver linings, but there are also hurricanes. There are wars, tragedies, and deaths, and the omnipresence of Jesus means that He is behind all these things. He is there, a patient, loving King, who is also gradually killing all of us as the wages of our sin. It is darned hard to feel good about that.

The omnipresence of Jesus, alone, is not a comfort but a terror. For this reason, I'd wager that most Christians don't actually believe in it. Instead, we tell ourselves that Jesus is only really hiding in all the places where we want to find Him. But the unfortunate side effect of this thinking is that while we're always searching for those God moments, those brief glimpses of what we like about God during our day, our days are mostly filled with the moments of God we don't like. Our lives are chock-full of times in which we believe that Jesus *is not*.

a patient, loving King is also gradually killing all of us

We are a lot like the deputies of Churchtown, then. We believe that whatever happened to the Ranger who was here long ago, He's gone now. Whatever the mission might have been, whatever answers might have found, whatever miracles He might have done, it's up to us now.

This is to our great detriment.

It doesn't matter what "lessons" we make up. The morals of the story will always be as diverse as the preachers preaching them. That is what happens when people make stuff up.

But what if there is more to the ascension than bare omnipresence? What if the omnipresence of Jesus' ascended body was only a stepping-stone to something more? What if His "filling all things" was not the end but only the beginning?

Mind Blown

It is to your advantage. (John 16:7)

JESUS, AS A SINGLE, male human, with a single, male, human brain, took on the job of sustaining the physics of every particle and atom scattered throughout the cosmos while simultaneously transcending time and space with His mind, ears, eyes, and more. But He didn't do it only to keep things going the same way they were before He died. As a man, He took on all power and authority and might from His Father for a reason. The Father gave the flesh and blood of Jesus the power of omnipresence in order for Him to do something very specific with it. Along with all authority in heaven and earth, Jesus also took to Himself the divine power to be in countless places at the same time while also retaining the human power to be in one place at one time.

Jesus of Nazareth ascended to the right hand of God so that He could permanently be with His Church in a way far more beneficial than merely sitting on a throne somewhere in Jerusalem. By Spirit and truth, with the intention to be in more than one place at one time, Jesus also has the power to choose how and where He wants His human body to become local again. Just as He could walk on water or appear in an upper room, just as He could vanish from the table of the Emmaus disciples yet appear to others miles away on that same day, so now, even more so, because He ascended to the Father, He can use the power of His omnipresence to be with His Church wherever two or three of us are gathered in His name.

Our modernized imagination has grown cold and stagnant. We no longer have the childlike wonder within us like they did in the ancient days of Churchtown. Back then, whenever the bandits came, the people stood firm, willing to be gunned down in cold blood, not because they believed that the Heavenly Ranger was gone but because they were convinced that the Heavenly Ranger was still with them. This was more than a mere presence in their memories or their hearts. This was *real*. This was a presence that only a man who was omnipresent would be able to be.

The ancient Christians were not willing to die because they believed that you could find the ascended Jesus anywhere and everywhere. They faced down their deaths boldly because they were convinced that they had found Jesus precisely *somewhere*. They held a firm conviction that Jesus' ascension achieved something far more marvelous than mere omnipresence.

Jesus can be in one place and multiple places at the same time

The good news of Jesus' ascension is that now He has the power to be in one place, and multiple places, at the same time. Please read that sentence again. Reigning at the right hand of God the Father, Jesus is the omnipresent "God the Son" without ceasing also to be the locally presentable "son of man" at the same time.

Because He is both, He can choose, as both, to be wherever and whenever He decides to be. The early Christians believed this, and they conquered the world with that belief. Their mission was not to convince one another that they could find Jesus if only they looked hard enough. Their mission was to share their conviction that they had already found Jesus. They believed that wherever they gathered together according to His commands, there **Jesus was with them**.

Deconstructing the Superstitions of Churchtown

The LORD brings the counsel of the nations to nothing. (Psalm 33:10)

WE SHOULDN'T be too hard on the silly sheriff and all his tomfool deputies who have come after him, parroting the doubts of the bandit-driven world. They've all thought they were after truth. They've all believed that what they were doing was going to help. How could they know that all of their unmasking of superstitions was actually the greatest superstitious endeavor of all?

The trick is that if you are going to safely do surgery on your brother's eye, nothing too huge can be obscuring your own. If you aren't careful, when you go to remove that speck from the guy next to you, you might just accidentally jam your finger into his eye socket. That is the real problem with logs in your vision. They are, by definition, blinding. Blind spots are, by definition, invisible, and invisible things are, by definition, obstacles you are incapable of knowing to be there.

So, when the sheriff and his doubts started Churchtown down that long, winding road of looking for the Heavenly Ranger somewhere other than in the midst of the town itself, he was unwittingly swallowing a major miscalculation. When he thought it was wise to point people to the memory of the Ranger rather than to the Ranger's substance, he was making an assumption that, while all too commonplace in its time, simply does not stand up to the tests of reality and history. Preaching "the remembrance" of Jesus as the antidote to Jesus' seeming disappearance, it turns out the "remembrance" is the very thing he was underestimating the most.

It wasn't God he doubted but God's **creation**. It wasn't faith that was lacking but **science**. It wasn't the essence of God's words that he most failed to consider but the essence of **words themselves**. 🖋

Where Has Jesus Been?

It is a matter of faith.

Hermann Sasse

God does not present us with any incomprehensible propositions.

Ulrich Zwingli

Who has made man's mouth?

I AM WHO I AM,
the God who brought Israel out of Egypt

Because I Say So

By the breath of His mouth . . . . (Psalm 33:6)

WORDS ARE things, and magnificent things at that. More than mere sounds, they are also more than mere meanings. Words are ideas made physical. They are thoughts in the flesh.

Words are a bridge, a fulcrum between thought and touch, a crux joining the material and the spiritual. From within us, they go out, incarnating the meaning within our minds into the fabric of the material world around us through the marvel of vibration, disturbance, and airflow. As a result, even the most obscure lie, the wildest superstition, or a far-flung fantasy, once it has become a string of words, is therefore as *real* as the sunlight on your skin.

This is science. When you speak, creation changes shape. It goes like this.

First, you have a thought. The edges of long strips of proteins and fats running through the gray matter of your brain begin to dance. Salts and acids zip about one another, freeing a charge of electricity to rush along one of millions of corrugated pathways. Imaging of these pulses appears as random lightning strikes flashing within the skull. But this is anything but random. It is phenomenal *design*. It is a pattern as mappable and trackable as the roads in your town. Only it is far more complex than any town or city on earth, not to mention more malleable. New roads are constantly opening. Old roads are ever closing off. Well-used roads rut and grow. Altogether they form a shifting, stabilizing superhighway of biochemical majesty, orchestrated as a living pattern that *is* your thoughts.

Some of these thoughts cause you to believe it is time to open your mouth and speak. Multiple lightning strikes fire and align to rush out the back of your neck and down chains of specialized wiring into the rest of your body. Some of it heads for the stomach, some for the lungs, some for the mouth and tongue. Branching out, they also all cohere in an intention so unified that before an eye can blink (indeed, in order for it to do so!), the fibrils of your muscles are

words are a bridge between material and spiritual

sparked by these flashing nerves. The electric current pulls directly on them, contracting and releasing multiple avenues at once to create movement.

In the case of speaking, it is a stunning composite. Throat, mouth, tongue, chest, and abdominals all weave together in simulation of those flickering ideas in your mind to mechanize the larynx just as enough wind is pressed over it to flood the mouth with noise that your teeth and lips then use to formulate a string of discernible sounds. At the very speed of thought, the thoughts become noise. Only this is not mere noise. These are *words*.

They are physical. From the mouth, the noises press out into the created world, as material as the book you are holding, as physically present as the atoms that make up its paper. There is nothing merely spiritual about them. Their presence is real, an alchemy of energy and mass that we call a *wave*.

Waves have *force*, which means that, though they may be invisible to the eye, they have the ability to be touched. If you've ever stood close to a speaker at a rock concert, or felt a sonic boom, then you know what I'm talking about. But in those same examples, the most important thing is not that you have the ability to touch the force of a wave. It is that the force of a wave has the ability to touch *you*.

A Quantum Ripple

I have uttered . . . things too wonderful
for me, which I did not know.
(Job 42:3)

WAVES ARE notoriously hyperactive things. Their essence is that they travel. Always. Yet subject to the laws of thermodynamics, just like a thrown football, waves do not travel forever. They only fly so far before the counterforces of friction or gravity compel them to stop. But where a football merely rests on the ground once the force of its throw has run out, the waves disperse their energy back into the molecules that have both carried and rubbed against them, until they are no more.

That is, sound can *die*. By nature, this glorious mystery of our firing brains working in harmony to send ideas given forceful form out into the world is a very frail thing. Words, as sounds, perish with their use.

Without this particular frailty, sound would not do us much good. We'd be trapped in a world of endless, amplifying forces, our brains overwhelmed by the onslaught. Thankfully, the God who created us had other plans in mind. He intended that within the limitations of sounds, and in the silence between them, something marvelous could take place: *communication*.

If I happen to be standing close enough to you when all those synapses fire and your breath blows the force of sound waves into the world around you, a second physiological miracle occurs: while the energized waves dematerialize by crashing into the created order, they also dematerialize and crash into me. I *feel* them.

We usually don't talk about feeling sound, unless, of course, we're too close to that speaker at the rock concert. Instead, we talk about "hearing." But hearing is just feeling on another level. To a very specialized part of your body, hearing *is* touch. By the power of that second, designed miracle, words are touch that you hear.

As those waves you have spoken push over me and past me, some of them are caught by oblong dishes sticking out of the side of my head. These bizarre little (or in my case, large) tools funnel that traveling sound force down a narrow canal that runs toward my brain. There, they run into my defense system, a very thin layer of skin stretched like a tarp across the mouth of the cave. It is small enough and tight enough that when the waves' sounds push against it, it moves, like a drum being struck by a mallet. The force of the wave is caught in what, to the eye, is an infinitesimal back-and-forth movement that is, in reality, incredibly hyperized.

hearing is just touch on another level

Energy is even further dispersed in the friction, allowing only a limited portion to press through and against a minute bone that rests against the tarp. The effect is much the same as when you put your hand against that speaker at the rock concert. Importantly, in this moment, the wave's force is no longer what we would call "sound." Now, thanks to your ear "drum," it has become *movement*.

Is This Insane Enough Yet?

Stand in awe. (Psalm 33:8)

THE LITTLE bone being moved by the reverberation of the drum is the first of three. These ear bones lean together in what amounts to a series of levers. As one moves, the others adjust, ever so slightly diminishing the movement's oscillation yet further. The last bone deftly presses against the outer membrane of another tender organ called the cochlea, a gnarly, shell-shaped enclosure filled with fluid. Like a long, spiraling pipe, its inner walls are papered with an extensive collection of hairs. Some are longer, others shorter—by only minute proportions to the naked eye but enough to determine massive differences in what happens next.

The now-soundless force that once upon a time was a lightning storm in my head now, through that lever system of bones in your head, exerts subtle pressure upon the fluid in your "inner ear," similar to when you gently squeeze a plastic bag filled with water. As the liquid fills the changing space between vibrations, moving this way a little, then that way back, the ebb and flow cause the little army of hairs to shift in the current like sea plants swaying on the ocean floor. As the lengths of the hairs differ, so some are moved more while others are moved less. Each of these twenty-some thousand individual extensions swaying in what remains of the sound wave is attached to its own personal fiber that extends through the cochlea wall and into another, larger pathway. These larger pathways join yet larger ones still, then again and again, linking every single microhair to the greater ethernet cable of your auditory nerve, itself quickly syncing up with the World Wide Web of your central nervous system.

By this point, the signal is no longer movement or force. What had once been energy in my mind has now become energy in yours, an electric impulse that will shortly shoot off lightning in your own brain, whether you like it or not. In the time it takes to blink, through a multiplex marvel of physics and chemistry, as that jolt runs up out of your cochlea and into your gray matter, flickering and spinning down the superhighway of your mind, the sounds I have mumbled are funneled down particular routes that you hold stored up as pens of *meaning*. My thoughts, become material noise, have now as material noise been received within you as your thoughts.

Whoa.

Jesus Is Still Here

Let Your steadfast love, O LORD, be upon us.
(Psalm 33:22)

THIS MEANS that the things we think of as "words," whenever we speak them and hear them, cannot help but physically alter your state of material existence. This is true whether we believe them or not. Unequivocally, scientifically, they move us. As sure as $E=mc^2$, words are real.

When I speak and you hear, you and I are tangibly connected. When you hear what I say, the unity created between us is not only spiritual. It is a physical, fellow-shaping of our minds. How much more true is this when I speak and you **believe** it!

Words are not ethereal. They are substance. They are part of the physical created order of our universe.

This means, then, that memory, too, is more than just memory. It is also real. It is also substance. Memory is a physical element of the past that remains in the physical present, an actual presence of that tremor in history that first created the thing remembered.

This in turn means that when Jesus, ascending into heaven, told His twelve apostles to "teach everything that I have commanded you, and therefore I am with you always, even to the end of the age" (cf. Matthew 28:20), He wasn't kidding.

There is no denying it. Even if we are only talking about the purely human element of His words, those truths are chemical, physical things that have remained with us today. They are a rebounding of His human, physical mind, bouncing back and forth through the bodies of one human after another all the way down the winding string of history. The accented syllables voiced by Jesus so long ago still carry to you His real, incarnate, human **presence** today.

words physically alter your material existence

To be sure, the same could almost be said of Julius Caesar or Plato, though that is somewhat like comparing a peewee baseball player to the big-league champ. In all that humanity has done, nothing has been remembered so often, with such regularity, with such ongoing, convicting, life-altering effect, as the repetition of the words of Jesus of Nazareth. More so still, among all such words of His, none have been repeated more frequently or with greater devotion than those He spoke in the Upper Room on the night He was betrayed. His human mind fired a lightning burst of synapses. His muscles twitched and sent that force flowing out from Him and onto others. "*Take. Eat. Drink. Do.*" A material ripple entered the universe, and it has not come close to stopping yet. Though His body has indeed ascended to the highest omnipresence, the same body can still also be felt, without a hint of transcendence, without a jot or tittle of omnipotence, breaking the expectations of fallen time and space with an ultimate movement that has also formed a common union among all the bodies of all the believers who have ever heard the echo of that night.

A Voice like God's

He spoke, and it came to be. (Psalm 33:9)

SOUNDS AS they fly through the air are, indeed, only symbols of the truths they contain. They are gibberish until they are heard. They are limited in their effect all the more until they are believed. But this hardly prevents them from being nothing more than noise. This hardly stops us from being able to communicate meaning.

But this is where that poor sheriff's error only began. Without even realizing the weakness of their claims, he helped those bandits establish a stronghold right beneath his nose. Assuming that the memory of the Heavenly Ranger was something **other than** His actual presence among them, he opened himself up to yet greater superstitions, while with the same stroke allowing the meaning of the Ranger's words themselves to be labeled superstition.

The slimmest degree of an angle, at its first point, seems only the fraction of a shift in direction. But once the path is traveled far enough, the lack of congruity

what if materialism is the real mythology?

becomes more and more clear. Eventually the new direction finds itself in uncharted waters that even the most radical of angles cannot outpace. Once in those waters, when the wind and storms begin to blow, so far removed from port, it is difficult to find the cause of the original error.

Yet this is the case for our age of the Church. Long before the postmodern bandits and revivalist hucksters could have their way with our town, we first had to allow ourselves to believe that the Ranger had left us. We first had to treat both His memory and His words as if they dwelt in the land of fantasy and imagination rather than in the material science of our practical lives. Adopting the belief that the ascension of Jesus meant that He was now more than a million miles away left us vulnerable to everything that has followed.

While you may not remember the time or place where this seemingly esoteric debate about His ascension took place, it's undeniable that it did. More so, it's my contention that the current buckling of Protestant Christianity is ultimately beneath the weight of this singular, unhappy error. When we, superstitiously and based strictly on human guesswork, denied to Jesus' words even their most primitive, incarnate power to be His presence in our midst, how could we expect anything less than the eventual denial of His Godhood as well?

Wouldn't you think that just as human words are demonstrably so much more than we assume, the words spoken by the God-who-became-flesh-in-order-to-speak-them must be at least that powerful? When the human synaptic lightnings and muscles and breath are also God's synaptic lightning and muscles and breath, should we not, at the very least, consider them to be a touch more substantial than the mere symbols the postmodern bandits claim of their own bantering words?

God never said "Let there be light" and then hoped that His suggestion might inspire understanding; much less did He sit waiting for someone else to infuse His speaking with their own personal meaning. He said, "Let there be light," and then the words themselves shone into being.

What if all created substance, before it was anything else, is first *words*? What if, when God is involved, words are more than mere sounds? What if words are the only real thing there ever is, or has been, or will be? 🌿

What More Could Jesus Do?

The claim that the greatest, most profound, and most all-encompassing community of human history has been established by these unimpressive-looking Sacraments is just as offensive to our thinking as is the assertion that God's Holy Spirit is given along this path. And yet this is the case. For this reason, the church herself remains an insoluble riddle for human reason, a pure article of faith.

Hermann Sasse

The question is, "Where is the Church?" What, therefore, are we to do? Are we to seek it in our own words or in the words of its Head, our Lord Jesus Christ? I think that we ought to seek it in the words of Him who is Truth, and who knows His own body best.

Augustine of Hippo

Let there be light.

God, the Father Almighty

No Safe Assumptions

> The natural person does not accept the things of the Spirit of God, for they are folly to him. (1 Corinthians 2:14)

HANGING nailed to a cross, we find God in all His glory. Who could believe such a thing?

No one, that's who. Despite ages of Old Testament prophecy, no one saw it coming. Despite years of face-to-face discipleship with a chosen band, no one believed the predictions. Despite the clarity of the New Testament documents, we hesitate to preach it still.

Because it's unbelievable. Gods don't die.

This is why we are obsessed with best practices. This is why we insist on changes in musical style. This is why I am actually concerned that some may question this chapter's doctrinal review, a process required by my church body's publishing system. Because when we find the Gospel is unbelievable, we choose to forfeit its unbelievability in order to build a more pragmatic approach to God.

Christianity's impossibility is its historical tenacity

Yet this is deadly.

It is within the Gospel's unbelievability that the true capacity of Christianity resides. It is because Jesus died *for us* and yet *against* our broken reason and strength that His death does us any good. It is Christianity's impossibility that is also its historical tenacity.

It is the preposterousness of Jesus' resurrection that makes it able to save us at all. If it were not unbelievable, it could not destroy unbelief. If it were reasonable, it could not be used by God to create faith alone.

Jesus Is As Jesus Does

> Who then is this? (Mark 4:41)

THIS IS the ultimate lesson of the cross. When a real God gets involved, it's only reasonable to start believing that all previously reasonable bets were off. You think God couldn't die? So what?

So what if humans don't rise from the dead? So what if everyone knows these things? In a world of bias, bugs, typos, and lies, self-evidence is only as reliable as the self who is assuming it. This is true without the cross, but the cross is God's everlasting exclamation point: *You don't get to make the rules.* *I do.*

In all that He did, Jesus of Nazareth demonstrated, time and again, that the only certain rule is that He does not play by our rules. He is the one who **made** them. He made them *for* us, as a gift. But if He wants to give us more gifts, new rules, then He is allowed to break the old rules whenever He wants to.

Jesus did impossible stuff all the time

As a result, one day Jesus stepped out onto a lake, and the water held Him up. He didn't need to change the water into ice or pad His feet with magical rubber. It was a **miracle**. God, as a man, did something impossible. He did something unbelievable. He did something that **cannot** be done. But as much as this boggled the minds of the confused people who saw it, this really wasn't a big deal for Jesus. As God made man, He did impossible stuff all the time.

He touched lepers without becoming unclean. Instead, His purity became the contagion. He handed out bread for lunch from loaves that never ran out, leaving behind more food than was there to begin with. He healed sick people whom He never met, from miles away. He got in a shouting match with the wind and brought it to heel like a whipped dog. He read minds with a look. On the night when He was betrayed, He . . .

Oh. Wait.

Sovereignty Gets Real

If you have faith . . . nothing will be impossible. (Matthew 17:20)

ISN'T IT fascinating that Christians of goodwill are not divided over whether or not Jesus fed five thousand or raised Jairus's daughter? I'm not talking about the miracle-denying, skeptical bandits. I'm talking about Bible-believing Christians who think Jonah was a real man and that Isaiah really prophesied the name "Cyrus." For such people, impossible things that Jesus did don't really bother us. Jesus is God. That makes Him Lord over all of nature. He can do with this world whatever He wills.

We treat every miracle in the Bible this way, from Moses parting the Red Sea to Peter healing a man with his shadow. There is nothing too radical, nothing too phenomenal for the God who made the universe.

Until.

Until you go and mention that one time when Jesus finished His last Passover meal, looked to His disciples with a new cup of wine in His hand, and spoke a timeless sentence so simple and yet so unbelievable that no naturally reasonable man can ever accept what it says.

"This is My blood."

How bizarre this must have been for Peter and the others. At this point, they didn't even believe that He was going to die for the sins of the world. How much less could they be ready to accept that the bit of bread that Jesus was handing them was at the same time a piece of His own flesh?

Naturally, the logical mind must dictate, without doubt or question, *the Lord meant this as a symbolic gesture. This was a moment of high idealism in which Jesus was trying to demonstrate by a word picture the revolutionary depths of what He was going to do next.*

If only Jesus were a man who did things naturally!

infinite Deity cooing as an infant defies all expectations

From the first day that the almighty and infinite Deity cooed as an infant, looking up in expectation for His virgin mother to change His diapers, Jesus of Nazareth has never been one to be limited to our expectations or understanding. Not a moment or word of Jesus' life failed to be utterly supernatural. Yet that is precisely the crisis of the question. For an arbitrary reason rutted in human traditionalism, this is where we draw the line.

Our doing so is anything but unreasonable. It is an order of the highest sensibility! It is also, and always has been, the root of everything that has ever divided us as Protestants. But rather than start with the divisiveness, rather than lay all our cards on the fact that for the first fifteen hundred years of Christianity's history, there was not a single, significant division over the meaning of Jesus' Last Supper words, let's first focus on something more inspirational. There is some good news about Jesus' words that will give us a place to start. For all our brokenness and the wide and raging whirlwind of crises that contemporary Christianity faces today, we are still united over at least one part of the phrase:

"Take and eat."

Fighting over Table Scraps

Ah, now You are speaking plainly and not using figurative speech! (John 16:29)

WHEREVER Christianity is found, in all its forms and varieties, with the exception only of those denominations that also deny the Trinity, all who remain committed to Jesus as the one true God also continue to take as institutional His exhortation to religiously repeat His words as well as to do them. Better yet, regardless of your tradition or private approach, when this taking and eating occurs, it's always considered one of the highest moments in Christian worship and devotion.

that all Christians still "take and eat" is radical

Some take it rarely, because they believe this enhances its meaning. Some take it often, because they believe its meaning enhances itself. But all take it. All recognize it as radically unique. All are aware that the words and actions themselves serve to set the entire event fully apart. If we take a moment to observe it, we will also see that among us all, it remains a singular mark that differentiates Christians from the rest of the world around us.

We should not underestimate what a ***radical impossibility*** this latter fact is, humanly speaking. No other human being has achieved such a dent in history. There have been many great men, from the august Caesars to the

Qin Dynasty, from Alexander to Genghis. Yet among all of them, prophets and kings, yogis and the Buddha, there has been no other human event, no birth or death, no victory or loss, so consistently ritualized with persistent devotion as the Last Meal of Jesus of Nazareth. For millennia, past empires and through chaos, amid direct persecution and between inadvertent swords, without regard to denomination or dogma, quarterly and weekly, less often and more, pious believers in Jesus gather in order to **believe** that He meant it when He said, "*Do this as My memorial.*"

This was Jesus' intention. It is no accident.

It also gives us a marvelously supernatural starting point for building agreement. Can you think of a more inspirational fact? In spite of all our fighting over truths, Jesus' institution remains a source of tremendous unity, and this should give us great hope.

this unity is no accident

We who believe that Jesus' death was not the end of Him but that He both rose from the grave and ascended to the seat of all authority may also boldly expect that the eating of bread and drinking of wine in His name will continue until the very end of the world. Better still, this means that we can expect that those churches which own this practice, which devote to it, also always have a future.

You can trust that the Church that has Jesus' Supper is a Church that cannot die. Yet this same hope comes with a more terrifying counterpart: a church that does not have Jesus' Supper is a church doomed to deteriorate and die, no matter how many other changes it swallows in the process.

Where Christ Is, There Is the Church

I will not leave you as orphans. (John 14:18)

TO TAKE away Jesus' marks of bread and wine is to take away Jesus Himself. It is to remove the ripple in history first started by His human words, which now have shown themselves capable of defeating history altogether. It is only mad expectations that could hope that such a hole in our boat would have no effect.

From this foundation, we must attribute to the meal a certain marvelous power to kill and make alive a congregation's faith. Whatever else you believe about the meaning of His words, the practice itself is its own proof. He spoke, and the words remain in our hearing. He gave the wine and we continue in the drinking. To hear, to participate, is to take a fellow-shape with Him through the religion He started. To cease, to refuse, to neglect, is to cut yourself off from what is self-evidently a most elemental part of being a Christian.

What could mere bread and wine do to conquer kingdoms? Nothing. How could such a plain, even boring, ritual outlast the pomp of all empires? It shouldn't. But it has. It does. It *will*.

This Sunday, once again, Christians the world over will gather to take and eat. For that holy hour the world dies to them and they die to the world. By the Supper itself we are set apart. Unbelievers do not do this. There is nothing here for the unbeliever to see. There is no God here to remember. There is only the taste of wheat and grape. But for the Christian, there is something more. According to Jesus' words "Do this," there is something to *believe*.

Whatever else might be made of it, like the power of human words themselves, this is more than mere symbol. Once again, like His words, we have in the action a real presence of the man who sat in that borrowed Upper Room with cup in hand and the first words on His lips.

Both His voice and His actions, sound waves and matter once made by the God who is man, have now danced through time and space to lift a cup to your lips, to press a promise against the drums of your ears, to enter into you with a meaning that cannot be disbelieved once the action is done.

Two thousand years after His death, Jesus has come to you to impact you, to enter you by word and deed, to segregate you from the world of unbelief. When you eat and drink, that is what you confess. "This meal is the work of Jesus."

to take away **Jesus' words** is to take away **Jesus**

Unavoidable Impact

Is it not a participation . . . ? (1 Corinthians 10:16)

ON THE NIGHT He was betrayed, Jesus said other magnificently potent, dynamically unbelievable things. But before we touch that discussion, we must come to grips with the simplicity of our lineage. Naked trust in the words "take and eat" has been the lifeblood of Christianity from the beginning. We should not be surprised that an era that has drastically limited their frequency is one that has also experienced tremendous atrophy.

your eating and drinking is the work of Jesus

Would you see revival? Would you have this Body of the Church rise from its sickbed? Then you must give heed to the heartbeat. You must find the place from which the blood will flow.

Christianity *is* trust in the radical, once-for-all uniqueness of Jesus. Our stand against the darkness can only prevail by embracing the reality that what He did on the night He was betrayed, He did entirely on purpose.

What More Could Jesus Have Said?

Scripture alone bears responsibility for the indisputably paradoxical nature of the assertions made in the eucharistic dogma. . . . A valid reason to depart from the literal understanding [ought] never be found in a philosophical argument against the possibility. . . . The one and only justification for abandoning the literal sense would be the existence of a word of Scripture that teaches a different understanding.

Hermann Sasse

Consequently, you can boldly address Christ both in the hour of death and at the Last Judgment: "My dear Lord Jesus Christ, a controversy has arisen over thy words. . . . I have remained with thy text as the words read. If there is anything obscure in them, it is because thou didst wish to leave it obscure, for thou hast given no other explanation."

Martin Luther

I appeal to you, brothers, by the name of our Lord Jesus Christ, that all of you agree, and that there be no divisions among you, but that you be united in the same mind and the same judgment.

Saul of Tarsus

Two Words

> This is why I speak to them in parables, because . . . hearing they do not hear, nor do they understand. (Matthew 13:13)

Τοῦτό ἐστιν

"This is."

So few words. So much division.

Whether you are confessional, questioning, charismatic, catholic, or church shopping, nothing has been more disruptive to your unity with the rest of world Christianity than the debate surrounding the meaning of these enigmatic words. It is only with shame that we must behold the shared mess of our Protestantism, like flotsam driven by a storm. But the greatest tragedy of all is that this catastrophic confusion was entirely avoidable. It did *not* have to be this way. The entire split could have easily been avoided, if not for the nearsighted misstep of one sadly thoughtless man.

Jesus.

No, not Luther. And no, not Calvin, Zwingli, or Wesley. Jesus.

I mean, come on. The guy is *omniscient*. He knows *everything*. This is the same guy who perceived and outwitted every last one of the Pharisees' word games without batting an eye. "Render unto Caesar!" and no one can argue with Him a single word. Don't you think that He might have spared five minutes to take a quick peek down the deep line of history and notice how disastrous His words about His Supper would turn out? He couldn't *not* know that He would be misunderstood.

But Jesus didn't do that. He knew everything, including how superstitious people can be. He knew how little His apostles understood almost everything He said in any parable or metaphor. But that didn't stop Him from sabotaging His prayer that we "all be one" with needlessly flowery language.

the only one to blame for this is Jesus

You don't have to like it. There is no question that it's downright embarrassing. The vast amount of wasted time and energy that could have been spared with only a few more words at the start is stunning. "This wine is red, like My blood is red, and the red will help you remember Me." There would have been nothing to doubt! "This bread is no longer bread. It is only the accidents of bread, but it is My body's substance." This, too, would have settled things right nicely.

The only one to blame for this is Jesus. There can be no question that He has all knowledge, which leaves us with the sad fact that He must have intended our divisions.

The Reason for Stories

I am speaking in human terms,
because of your natural limitations.
(Romans 6:19)

MATTHEW, Luke, and Mark really botch it up as well. With great consistency, they take pains in every place to make sure that we understand: "He put another parable before them"; "He told them another parable"; "All these things Jesus said . . . in parables." Yet here, they lead us astray.

Well beyond parables themselves, the authors of Scripture are at pains to explain Jesus' words and avoid confusion. There is that time when Jesus was in the courtyard, shouting about tearing down the temple. Everyone there misunderstood Him. But St. John clears it all up for us by pointing out that He was talking about His own body and His crucifixion (John 2:19–21). Then there is that time when Jesus got a bit eccentric about finding a very particular donkey. Thankfully, Matthew is swift to point out that there was a good explanation for this. "This took place to fulfill what was spoken by the prophet," he points out, giving the reference (Matthew 21:4). Even Agabus, the unsung seer of Ephesus, after wrapping Paul's belt around his hands and feet as a prophetic children's sermon illustration, is clear to *explain* what it means. "This is what will happen to Paul," he says (cf. Acts 21:10–11).

Such explaining is in good company. Jeremiah does not merely break a flask in the sight of the people as a symbol of what God is going to do to them. He interprets the metaphor. "Thus says the LORD of hosts: So will I break this people" (Jeremiah 19:11). Ezekiel does the same with the watchmen. Isaiah does the same with the vineyard. Hosea does the same with Gomer.

Even the marvelous "I am" statements of John, often trotted out as a vaunted one-move checkmate to prove once and for all that it's possible for Jesus to use symbolic language, only prove that Jesus was ingrained in the habit of explaining His symbols.

I am the vine; you are the branches. [*And by this I mean that*] Whoever abides in Me . . . bears much fruit. (John 15:5)

I am the door. [*And by this I mean that*] If anyone enters by Me, he will be saved. (John 10:9)

I am the good shepherd. [*And by this I mean that*] [I lay] down [My] life for the sheep. (John 10:11)

I am the resurrection and the life. [*And by that I mean that*] Whoever believes in Me, though he die, yet shall he live. (John 11:25)

I am the way, and the truth, and the life. [*And by this I mean that*] No one comes to the Father except through Me. (John 14:6)

Yet here we are, on this most precarious evening, surrounded by the more grave and reverent ancient rituals of Israel, praying with drops of blood that nothing in heaven or earth could divide these men, and Jesus goes silent. The apostles go silent.

Stark.

Stunningly void.

Intentionally obscure.

τοῦτό ἐστιν

Matthew: "This is My body" (Matthew 26:26). *Period.*
Mark: "This is My body" (Mark 14:22). *Period.*

St. Paul rides to our aid! "This is My body, *which is for you*" (1 Corinthians 11:24).

But that's not much help. "For you" is not an explanation. It's a direction.

Paul, and Luke with him, then also adds the highly praised "Do this in remembrance of Me." Yet this, too, is not an explanation. It is a command, one that no true Christian on earth has ever questioned or avoided.

what use is a metaphor without a meaning?

When Paul then goes on to tell us that the entire Supper is given to "proclaim the Lord's death until He comes" (1 Corinthians 11:26), he at least is giving us an insight into what the ritual meal *does*. But "do" as it might, we still have no idea *how*. We have a symbol without clear significance. We only have a metaphor without a *meaning*.

An Empty Image

> Like a lame man's legs, which hang
> useless, is a proverb in the mouth of fools.
> (Proverbs 26:7)

A METAPHOR requires a point of contact. The definition of a metaphor is the combination of two connected ideas in order for one to explain the other. But how do eating bread and drinking wine proclaim Jesus' atoning death? It's popular to say that Jesus' Supper is about remembering Him. But how bread and wine actually achieve this is left unasked, and therefore unanswered.

It is possible to point to Jesus' death as the proper explanation of the ancient symbolism of the Passover lamb. Just *like* the lamb was slain in a transaction to remove the judgment on sin, so Jesus was also crucified as a vicarious satisfaction of the wrath of God against us. This symbol makes sense. It has a contact point. It allows one image to explain the other. But how are the bread and wine just *like* Jesus' body and blood?

A few say that by reenacting the Supper, faith is generated to ascend to heaven and spiritually feast on Jesus there. This is a pious thought! But it is far from a popular teaching. In fact, it has become downright obscure. Neither does it answer our question: How does the image of bread and wine do any such thing?

Others say that eating Communion, even alone in a back corner while the rock band plays on, engenders a personal, spiritual experience of Jesus' *suffering*. This sounds very nice and meek. But it cannot counter the assertion that it's not suffering but ***becoming new*** that is represented. Others find all these former suggestions a bit flat, contending that the bread and wine demonstrate the ***ethics*** of Jesus' self-sacrificial personality. Yet more prefer less highbrow responses, noticing that the wine is ***red***, just like blood. Blood is red, just like wine. Boom. Symbolism!

The problem, of course, is that bodies aren't much like bread in color. The answer to this has been to lean hard into the word *broken*, as in He "took bread, and after blessing it ***broke*** it and gave it" (Matthew 26:26, emphasis added). After all, Jesus knew that His body was about to be broken the next day. So He wanted the bread to be a picture of His ***breaking***. That sounds good, right? Except that it's about as unbiblical as one can get. There is no question that this kind of image feels very meaningful as the pastor hands you a piece of bread, saying, "The body of Christ, ***broken*** for you," but the body of Jesus was ***never*** broken. Jesus suffers. Jesus is scourged. Jesus is stricken, smitten, and afflicted. Yet St. John goes out of his way to explain (yet again!) that in everything done to Jesus—the spitting, the hating, the piercing—Jesus' body ***not breaking*** in the midst of it was a direct fulfillment of prophecy (see John 19:36).

Does Jesus break the bread? Yes. But reading a deeper metaphorical meaning into the action, while sincere, is also purely arbitrary. Is the chewing also a symbol? ***Why not?*** What about the use of a single cup? the lack of leaven? having the meal at night? in an upper room? with only men participating? It's a never-ending rabbit hole of personal assumptions.

Jesus breaks the bread, and then He distributes it. People chew and swallow it. This is highly normal behavior. But He then speaks highly ***abnormal*** words. The words themselves say nothing of the breaking. In the place where many pastors today will say "broken," Jesus Himself says "***given***."

I'm not trying to mince words. I'm trying to anchor our faith in something greater than novelty. God made each of us clever enough to make up something symbolic and meaningful in a given moment. We all did it in grade school. "Johnny, describe how Bobby is like a tiger." It's easy.

But since Jesus is the one making up a symbol, shouldn't we want our understanding of it to be the same as His? Can we not find a single meaning that is authentically and everlastingly correct? Do we not want to *mean* what Jesus *meant*?

Yet we have no single, clear explanation from Him or His apostles. No matter how meaningful or clever we might feel about our pet answers, all our explanations crumble into a jumbled pile of (very divided) opining around a word picture without any clear purpose. This is a serious problem.

Five hundred years of arguing about it has left its share of suggested answers, but an abundance of shots in the dark is not the issue. The challenge is that no single meaning has ever risen to the top of the pile. The only thing that has become certain is that whatever the symbol of the Lord's Supper might mean for you or for me, it clearly doesn't mean that for everyone else. They have their own meanings.

If the only point of agreement we have is that Holy Communion is a symbol, then it is sad symbolism indeed. All that it can serve to represent is precisely how vast and wide our divisions actually are. If Jesus knows everything, Jesus should have known this would happen. If "this is" *is* a metaphor, then it's one of the most costly and willfully obtuse linguistic blunders in the history of the world. 🐾

if Holy Communion
is a symbol,
then it is
sad symbolism
indeed

What Did Jesus Actually Say?

The cause of strife . . . does not lie in the Lord's Words but in the doubt of people who do not want to believe him in these words.

Hermann Sasse

Seeing, touching, tasting—are in thee deceived; How says trusty hearing? That shall be believed! What God's Son has told me, take for truth I do. Truth himself speaks truly, or there is nothing true.

Thomas Aquinas

Be still, and know that I am God.

YHWH, David's Lord

Unlike a Simile

> Let Us go down and there confuse their language, so that they may not understand one another's speech. (Genesis 11:7)

BUT WHAT if Jesus actually did want to say something as insane as "Hey, everybody, this bread right here in My hand is also My human body"? Forget the philosophy for a moment. Just ask the linguistic question.

If Jesus wanted to convey some miraculous-impossible-super-divine way of being a piece of bread, what other words should He have said instead? Which words could He have used? Could Jesus have added an "also" or an "in My hand"? Sure. But if a dynamic verb like "is" is not enough, is an adverb or a prepositional phrase really going to change your mind?

I can just see it now:

Jesus: Hey, guys. Guess what? Eat this. This is My body. Cool, huh? And this cup—

Peter: Slow down there, Jesus. I don't get it. It sounded like You just said that the bread there in Your hand is kind of like Your body in some metaphorical way. But You didn't tell us how. Please explain to us the parable.

Jesus: No, Peter. I meant what I said. I'm not speaking to you in parables. This isn't that "leaven of the Pharisees" stuff here. I'm saying that this bread *is* My body.

Thomas: But Jesus, that doesn't make any sense. Your body is sitting right there, holding the bread. Besides, if this bread is Your body, then how come it still looks like bread and tastes like bread? It didn't bleed when You broke it just now.

Jesus: Because, Thomas, this thing in My hand *is* still bread too, but that bread *is* My body also.

Phillip: Sorry, Jesus. This sounds like more of that crazy talk that got people all riled up in Capernaum. You're only going to confuse people speaking this way. But I think I know what You're really

what if Jesus wanted to say something insane?

getting at and how to say it better. When those guys write about this, they should say it like this: after You die tomorrow (which none of us believe will happen, by the way), once You rise from the dead and ascend into heaven, leaving us here to die miserable, horrible deaths at the hands of Your enemies, what You intend is that our strict and mindless obedience to eating the bread and drinking wine while repeating Your words verbatim, but not technically believing them, will comfort us with technically not-believing faith as it spiritually ascends to feast on the idea of Your total sovereignty over everything in the universe—except, You know, the ability to be that piece of bread if You want to, right? I mean, that makes a **ton** more sense.

Jesus: (*Sighs.*) I'm at a loss here, guys. I was worried about something like this happening when I cursed human language way back at Babel. But it's not like I'm trying to explain quantum mechanics here. I'm only asking that you trust Me beyond what you can see. When have you ever asked Me to explain a miracle? I mean . . . (*Throws up His hands.*) Look, there really isn't any other way to say what I'm saying. This bread is My body. That's as clear as I can be. Tell you what. Let's wait until Pentecost, and then we'll talk it over again, all right?

It "Is" the Copula

Your word is a lamp. (Psalm 119:105)

NOT TO BE crass about it, but *is* is sex for words. It combines meanings in an intimate, mysterious way, in order to procreate our understanding of the things we're talking about. Even in its weakest form, the metaphor, *is* is always a verbal fusion, a powerful utterance insisting that two things that are not the same are indeed the same after all. That's why those old-school grammarians with their wooden rulers for your knuckles used to call it the "copula." *Is* **copulates** ideas.

Every human language that exists has a way to do this. A few ancient, "caveman speak"–style languages, like Hebrew, technically hide the copula. *Gordo strong! Gordo wise!* But this is not because they do not have *is*. They only consider *is* to be so basic and obvious that there is no need to bother verbalizing it. We do much the same thing today when we hide *is* behind an apostrophe *s*.

So when the ancient Gordo, son of Hemalikiah, would talk about this or that without ever saying the word *is* out loud, the minds of those around him natively understood that the *is* was there. Because Gordo cannot **do** wise or **eat** wise or **run** wise, he must **be** wise, or at least consider himself so.

This geek-deep dive into linguistics is important for Jesus' Words of Institution. Both Hebrew and Aramaic, languages Jesus would have spoken as mother tongues, function with the silent copula. If Jesus was speaking either of these languages in the Upper Room, He could not have possibly said out loud, "This **is** My body," because there is no way to say "is" in either tongue. Instead, He would have had to say, "This, My body."

For some, this is the silver bullet needed to end all conversation on the meaning of His words. In one fell swoop, all contention for the bread actually "being" Jesus comes collapsing down. All those years of Church tradition and theology that say otherwise are based on words that aren't even there in the original!

Of course, aside from thereby making the claim that Hebrew could only ever speak in metaphor and had no way to say real things, it more dangerously also means that Scripture, alone, is **not** what we are to put our trust in. Rather, we should trust in the New Testament only after it has been back-translated into Hebrew, assuming to ourselves the power to infallibly translate it. At the same time, we must therefore distrust the capability of the apostles to translate what Jesus said into the Greek language, since that is what they did, and it is their words that we are running to other languages in order to ignore.

"*is*" **is copulation for words**

Hypothetical Backflips

> He will take what is Mine and declare
> it to you. (John 16:15)

IT'S IMPORTANT to make it clear that we don't know what language Jesus spoke in the Upper Room. This argument is in many ways an exercise in imagining things. But it's also a great proving ground for testing the way we read the Scriptures.

For the moment, let's grant the argument that Jesus spoke Aramaic on that night in the Upper Room. If such were the case, then there is no choice but to believe that the authors of the New Testament then chose to translate what He said into Greek. When they did so, for some bizarre reason, they *inserted* the copula. They added the word *is* to Jesus' words. You might think, "Of course they did. They had to translate the metaphor." But this is just the thing: the Greek *does not* need to have "is" inserted at all.

Greek is a real odd duck of a language. Greek likes to have its cake and eat it too. In the common Greek of Jesus' day, Gordo, son of Hemalikiah, would have been free in any conversation to have his pick. He could say, "Gordo wise," or he could say, "Gordo **is** wise." It all depended on how he felt, or what kind of hurry he was in. It is just the same freedom you have today to say either "It is" or "It's." No one in the room misses a beat whatever you decide. We don't even think about it.

the apostles made a real muck of things

But *if* Jesus instituted the Supper in Aramaic and *therefore* couldn't use the word *is* as God's way of enshrining the meaning of His words in permanent metaphor, then when the apostles translated it into common Greek, they really made a muck of things. Rather than translate it literally and woodenly, as they were perfectly capable of doing, rendering "This, My body" into Greek, they instead took the pains to *add* a physical word.

More! They did not add the word *symbolizes*, although they could have, and I would argue they should have if that is what was meant. Nor did they add the word *represents*, nor the phrase *is like*, nor *is as if*. Instead, all four of the writers, very intentionally, took Jesus' Aramaic meaning to be most clearly carried into Greek by inserting the lonely copula. Under inspiration of the Holy Spirit, they wrote, "This **is** My body."

Frankly, I know not nor care if Jesus spoke Aramaic in the Upper Room. If it matters to you, that's great. I don't mind if you believe either way. But I do mind when faithful, wise, otherwise Bible-believing Christians become so committed to their position on what Jesus must have meant that they willingly jettison trust in the inspiration and inerrancy of the Scriptures themselves, and instead grasp for "what if" proofs, refusing to read what the Scriptures clearly write things "are."

Seriously.

All that our opining can do is divide us further. Pious subtleties that undermine the trustworthiness of the actual words Jesus has instituted and left us shall never unify us. We must either take the writings we have received from the apostles as the ones Jesus wants us to have, or we must believe that Jesus does not want us to have any specific words at all. Flying above, around, or behind the text always has only one end. Doubting the verbal inspiration of the Bible will always also mean doubting the **meaning** of the Bible.

I am not contending that Christians who are committed to a symbolic or spiritual understanding of Christ in the Supper intend to undermine the inerrancy of the Bible. But at least so far as the current example argument is concerned, that is exactly what has happened, and all to no avail but further division.

The Legacy of a Misstep

Why did you doubt? (Matthew 14:31)

IF JESUS wanted His words to be taken as a picture or metaphor, then we must admit this much: they are a vague and disruptive symbol. If their meaning is not plain, then there is no clear meaning to them at all. But if Jesus really wanted to give us a simple statement of a miraculous reality, He used the only word that human language has given us for making such claims. He could not have said it any other way, nor did He.

In a Bible where Jesus often explains parables but never explains miracles, "it's impossible" is a terribly poor argument against His plain meaning. More than terrible, it has been historically cataclysmic. For once we started down this nonbiblical path of judging the Scriptures by our understanding, we could only eventually find ourselves subsumed beneath the reign of doubt.

Why not question the reality of Jonah? Who is to stop us from questioning a tall tale about five pieces of bread and two fish, or walking on water, or rising from the dead? Once Scripture is subjected to what we are willing to believe possible, what *is* means quickly becomes the least of our worries. By the time we are done applying our doubts to the rest of the Bible, next to nothing is left. We flee from doubting "is" to doubting "often" to doubting "wine" to doubting "forgiveness."

It should not surprise us that after giving such thinking pride of place for so long, skeptical minds have moved on to questions about "six days" and "marriage" and "sin" and "hell." It's not a wonder that the license to doubt has led to versions of Christianity that preach not only a symbolic supper but a symbolic death of the Son of God.

"it's impossible" is a terribly poor argument

What remains now is this unfortunate truth: *there is no passage of Scripture that teaches us to question the Scriptures*. Yet there are countless passages that insist on its perspicuity. The Bible, indeed, says many things. But "God cannot do what He says" is not one of them.

If we are to have any hope in surviving the doubt-driven decline storming over the sides of our little boat, we can no longer assume for ourselves old assertions, inferences, and speculations. We now stand face-to-face with the wrath of God against an unbelieving culture, pressed down under cover of deep darkness. From two thousand years ago, Jesus Himself sits with us, staring across the table with eyes fully aware of the sweaty, bloody terror that shortly awaits Him. He only has a few moments left, a few more words to say.

"This is" is what He left us. ✤

What Did Paul Receive?

It is not a superfluous quarrel among theologians, but a necessary battle for the church's preservation.

Hermann Sasse

Come together man by man, in common, through grace, individually, in one faith . . . with an undivided mind, breaking one and the same bread, which is the medicine of immortality, and the antidote to prevent us from dying, but [which causes] that we should live forever in Jesus Christ.

Ignatius of Antioch

For My thoughts are not your thoughts . . . declares the LORD. . . . So shall My word be that goes out from My mouth; it shall not return to Me empty, but it shall accomplish that which I purpose.

Isaiah, son of Amoz

Before There Were Scriptures

> They devoted themselves to the apostles' teaching and the fellowship, to the breaking of bread. (Acts 2:42)

CHRISTIANS had the Lord's Supper before they had the New Testament. This is indisputably true so long as by "New Testament" you mean the books of the Bible. Jesus' resurrection gathered Christians from Jerusalem to Judea to the edges of the Roman Empire for nearly two decades without a single word of it being written down.

Of course, this doesn't mean that they did not have the New Testament as the Bible defines it. This only means that they did not have a set of *documents* recording it. But they certainly had the *substance* of a better and newer covenant established between God and man in the body of the one man Jesus Christ.

Long before anything was written down, whether coming from the mouth of Peter or Paul, James or Apollos, these unified words from Jesus, about Jesus, rang forth. Everything that He had taught His apostles was carried forward in clear and memorable words, a sound and sufficient "pattern" (2 Timothy 1:13) of "teaching," or διδαχή (di-da-kay). This was the Church's *doctrine*, what the first Christians *knew* to be true, even without having it written.

Even more important is that not all of this διδαχή was created equal. Yes, it was all true. But not all of it held the same place in the lives of the Christians who were instructed in it. All of it was confessed and believed with equal dedication but not with equal repetition. As Christians came together to receive and remember the words of the Lord, some words were spoken more often than others.

We've already acknowledged this in previous chapters, but what is important to add now is that of all the words that were repeated, and then repeated again, and then eventually written down, very few of them actually contain the term "New Testament." In all the New Testament documents we've received, the phrase not only shows up merely a handful of times, but it only shows up *once* in the mouth of Jesus Himself.

Is it only an accident that the only recorded moment in which Jesus mentions the "New Testament" also happens to be the single most quoted and celebrated set of words in all the words He ever said? From that first Pentecost onward, His statement about "the New Testament in [His] blood," [1] spoken around and with bread and wine in remembrance of Him, was *the* event that called Christians out of their homes, into streets and catacombs, away from the Hebrew temple and out of the synagogues. There were many other things Jesus said, much διδαχή spoken and passed on, but the words of "the New Testament" were the glue that bound everyone together into the present thing called "Church."

This is dynamic. Before there was the Bible to hold us together, there was our Lord's Supper. The Church of Jesus Christ existed for decades without New Testament Scriptures, but we did not exist for a single week without the New Testament of Jesus' Holy Supper. This institutional Meal was so effective, so powerful, that the apostles managed to go on for decades trusting in its sufficiency alone, never feeling a whit of pressure to write any of it down!

before there was the Bible, there was the Lord's Supper

That day did come. By then the churches had spread so that they existed in places so far-off that it was humanly impossible for an actual apostle to be present at all times. It was in such places, during such absences, that some no doubt well-meaning Christians began teaching a word or two of their own. They began teaching things that Jesus had not quite said, or without realizing it, they misconstrued the words He had said. These were the events that finally compelled the apostles to take up pens and clarify Jesus' words.

---

1   1 Corinthians 11:25, ESV: "covenant"; the Greek διδαχή (di-da-kay) can easily be rendered as both "testament" and "covenant." The emphasis here is to recognize that 1 Corinthians 11:25 is one of only a handful of places in the New Testament where the phrase "New Testament" occurs. This cannot be accidental so far as the early Christian understanding of the words is concerned.

The First Letters

Write what you see in a book and send it. (Revelation 1:11)

EVERY LETTER that today we call the "New Testament" comes about in order to deal with the divisive threat of false teaching. By the year AD 55, Saul of Tarsus, also known by his Greek name "Paulos," had written at least four letters confronting "different doctrines" or ἕτερο-διδαχή (heh-ter-o-di-da-kay), later known as "heterodoxy," with the ὀρθό-διδαχή (or-thoe-di-da-kay), the "orthodoxy" or "straight doctrine" of Jesus' words and their instruction.

The first letter, sent with haste to the region of Galatia, was inspired by the same events that triggered the first churchwide crisis and resulting Council. This massive meeting was an unprecedented event in the life of the Early Church. Along with establishing textual study and conversation as the New Testament pattern for reconciliation on matters of truth, it also stands as the moment of clean break between rites of the old covenant and those of the new.

Within a year or so of that Council, Paul rushed off two more short letters. Both of them were sent to the same congregation in the far north: Thessalonica. There, a number of bizarre new heterodoxies cropped up regarding the end of the world.

After this, the apostle's pen went silent for nearly five years. It wasn't as though he were taking it easy. Paul went on two massive missionary journeys. Everywhere he visited, a complex mixture of controversy and conversion followed him. Without the New Testament Scriptures, but with the practice of the Lord's Supper firmly established as a binding root, he planted numerous congregations, including one in the eclectic little port city of Corinth.

Paul spent over a year with the Corinthians. In this city, nestled in a waterway on the southern edge of the Grecian peninsula, he developed strong ties while toiling with his hands as a tentmaker and leatherworker. Yet, at some point, he decided that the New Testament "traditions" (1 Corinthians 11:2) were well enough established that he could move on, eventually making his way back to the Holy Land. Once there, he could hardly sit still before he embarked on yet another missionary adventure.

This time, his plan was to revisit many of the young congregations he'd left behind on previous journeys. This included Corinth. But the Lord, it seemed, had other ideas.

While Paul was passing through the city of Ephesus, a great door for work was opened to him. Unexpectedly, within an extremely brief amount of time, such a drove of people began converting to Christianity that it actually buckled the local economy! The city was built in part on a strong silver trade, focused significantly on the manufacture of metal idols. The many conversions, by putting a dent in the idol business, also put a dent in the metal business. Needless to say, the events surrounding this, including a particularly nasty run-in with a smith named Demetrius, kept Paul quite busy. As a result, he was delayed from the rest of his planned journey.

We do not know if it was this delay that led Paul to send his first letter to Corinth or some other matter. In fact, we know almost nothing about his first letter. This is *not* the 1 Corinthians that we now confess as part of the Bible; it is an earlier epistle he wrote and sent from Ephesus. All that we know about this letter is that Paul mentions it *within* 1 Corinthians (5:9). Because of that reference, we also know that at least a portion of it had something to do with the dangers of public immorality.

Whatever else the letter might have said or not said, it did not have its intended effect. Unbeknownst to him, ἑτερο-διδαχή had already well planted itself among the Corinthians. Such a foothold was established that over the next few years, Paul would write *three* more letters, as well as make one emergency trip away from Ephesus when it became clear that the letters were not working as he had hoped.

I can easily imagine being St. Paul, embroiled in a sociocultural battle against Demetrius and his crony quasi-political mafioso, rejoicing at the Baptisms and conversions happening day by day but also deeply concerned with preparing these new Christians for the very real physical persecution on the horizon. I can imagine him jotting off a quick "I'm sorry I won't be visiting like I'd planned, but remember not to do bad stuff" letter, relying on the fond memories of the people to whom he wrote and convinced they would take it like good friends are wont to do. I can imagine him reeling from confusion when a letter returns from them, delivered by some of their own members, stamped with the names of the most prominent families, and fluxing in content somewhere between "What did you mean?" and "Who do you think you are to speak to us this way?"

We do not have a copy of this letter. We only have Paul's *response* to it in the book we now call 1 Corinthians. Though the letter itself doesn't say so, the history shows that the situation was something of an urgent shock for St. Paul. He put 1 Corinthians directly into the hands of his long-term friend, trainee, and traveling companion, a man whom he called his own son,

Timothy. Whatever else might be said, to Paul this growing rift in Corinth, after the Galatian controversy of many years before, was the greatest threat fledgling Christianity had yet faced.

Before, in Galatia, the Gospel itself had been under attack from the broken teaching of works-righteousness. In Thessalonica, the Gospel was muffled beneath disorienting falsehoods regarding the end of the world and Jesus' return. Now the Gospel was under attack at the very place those two teachings came together: What is happening when we eat bread and drink wine together as *the* New Testament?

What happens when the place where we "proclaim the Lord's death until He comes" (1 Corinthians 11:26) and receive a cup "for the forgiveness of sins" (Matthew 26:28) becomes the battleground of personal ambition, sexual license, and me-centered spirituality?

Clearly the issue was severe enough that another casual visit "after passing through Macedonia" (1 Corinthians 16:5) wasn't going to cut it. This called for more than "some spiritual gift" (Romans 1:11) to be imparted. With the New Testament itself now all but removed from among them ("It is not the Lord's Supper that you eat" [1 Corinthians 11:20]), it was time for these words of the Lord to be *written down*.

Letter to the Corinthians, Chapter 1: Total Mind Body

> You who once were far off have been brought near by the blood. (Ephesians 2:13)

In 1 Corinthians, Paul will use the word *body*, or σῶμα (so-mah), *forty-six* times! The book, for all its varied topics, is a barrage of repetition, a string of beacons for careful readers to follow. Whatever διδαχή is tied up in Paul's concern that the Corinthians learn to discern "the body" (1 Corinthians 11:29) of Jesus, it's as if he desires to make that point by force of will. There is countless ἑτερο-διδαχή to deal with, from divisions over personalities and disagreements about culture to opinions about sexuality and inconstant rules for buying groceries, from worship events disrupted by vanity to a willful neglect of the resurrection of Jesus. But it's clear to Paul that all of these problems stem from a single, forgotten truth: that to be the Christian Church means that "you are the body of Christ" (1 Corinthians 12:27).

The reason that there should be "no divisions among you" (1 Corinthians 1:10a) is because "you are the body of Christ." The reason we are to be "united in the same mind and the same judgment" (1 Corinthians 1:10b) is because "you are the body of Christ." The reason that Christians "are not lacking in any gift" (1 Corinthians 1:7) is because "you are the body of Christ."

This is no offhanded turn of phrase or philosophical pretty language. This is a *first principle* of Christianity. All the other false assumptions and flawed practices in Corinth flow from a failure to believe *this*. Forty-six σῶμας will soon come barreling toward us in order to insist upon it.

Paul uses the word *body* forty-six times

But what does *this* mean?

To our spiritualizing, modern ears, "you are the body" sounds like some generalized appeal to kindness, or perhaps awareness of unity amidst our diversity. This leads us to hear Paul's words about being "united in the same mind" as some appeal to consensus building, or agreeing to disagree. Lost on us is the tremendously *physical* nature of his language. Easily missed is the powerful fact that having "the **mind** of Christ" (1 Corinthians 2:16, emphasis added) is substantially more than a merely spiritual reality.

Jesus of Nazareth, dead and raised, *is still human*. He is still a *material man*. That means that, whatever super-important and awesome truths His mind might contain, "the mind of Christ" is still a single man's *physical brain*. His thoughts (which are not your thoughts) are also a flickering bundle of neurons, flooded with hemoglobin and pulsing under the feeding of a blood-laden heart. That heart beats in the chest of the same body that once lay in a manger in Bethlehem but is also now scarred where it was pierced with a spear. Now, risen from the dead and ascended to the highest heaven, He, the man, is both managing the entire universe *and*, by the majesty of the incarnation, also using a pile of gray matter to do it.

The "mind of Christ" that we have is the **tactile, human brain of God**.

Don't ask me how. That's the point. We don't know how to be God. We don't know how to do what God does. We don't get to set rules and limitations for Him. If we want to know who He is, or what He thinks, or how He reigns, then the only way we know any of it at all is because He deigns to tell it to us.

The incarnation of the eternal, begotten Son as an eternal, now dead and risen man is meant to be a divine mystery on every level. It is meant to be an article of *faith*. Whatever hidden addiction you might have to science and proofs and logic, articles of faith exist to destroy that misplaced allegiance. Articles of faith exist in order to **not** be understood so that they have to be *believed*.

Letter to the Corinthians, Chapters 1–2: The Wisdom of Not Knowing

How unsearchable are His judgments! (Romans 11:33)

YOU DO NOT get to explain how the infinity of God dwells within the finitude of a single man. You do not get to figure out how virgins give birth or how men walk on water. The cavalier and impious boast "I can't wait to get to heaven and ask God to explain the Trinity to me" is brazen ignorance.

The ***Gospel fact*** is that there are truths that we will never understand. But standing at the center of all those truths is a man who is understanding *embodied*. He doesn't just speak the διδαχή. He *is* the διδαχή. In His ***body***. Forever. Heaven and earth may pass away, but the body of Jesus, "the body of Christ," will not.

This is why Paul's insistence that "you are the body of Christ" is so imperative. "You are **in**" Him (1 Corinthians 1:30, emphasis added). This is no fluffy, pious talk. Having "the mind of Christ" is not an appeal to niceness. The religion of Jesus is the same things ***as*** Jesus. Jesus *is* ***Christ***ianity.

You might prefer the charm of Apollos or the stability of Cephas (1 Corinthians 3:22), but it's the pulsing of the neuro-pathways of Jesus that matter. You might love eating bacon or prefer fewer saturated fats, and that's no big deal at all (see 1 Corinthians 10:25). If "Crispus and Gaius" (1 Corinthians 1:14) go left and the members of "the household of Stephanas" (1 Corinthians 1:16) go right, we can handle it like brothers. But what Christianity absolutely ***cannot*** tolerate is letting such merely human decisions cloud the ***common union*** we share with ***physical*** mind of our God.

"I appeal to you, brothers, by the name of our Lord Jesus Christ, that all of you agree, and that there be no divisions among you, but that you be united in the same mind and the same judgment" (1 Corinthians 1:10). This is no flowery language. This is flesh and bone.

Tangible.

Particular.

"Crucified" (1 Corinthians 1:23).

"The power of God and the wisdom of God" (1 Corinthians 1:24).

Nailed to a tree.

the pulsing of the neuro- pathways of Jesus

Neurons darkened and synapses failing to fire beneath a sun that refused to shine.

"What is weak . . . what is low and despised . . . even things that are not" (1 Corinthians 1:27–28), now glorified, high and lifted up, filling all the things that ever are.

"Jesus Christ and [His body] crucified" (1 Corinthians 2:2) is *the* διδαχή. The ultimate wisdom is a dead body nailed to a tree. Who among us can claim to be wise? "No [bodily] eye has seen, nor [physical] ear heard, nor the [beating] heart of man imagined" (1 Corinthians 2:9) such a marvel. We are not capable of such thoughts. But He *is* the eternal "thoughts of God" (1 Corinthians 2:11). He is the eternal mind manifested into eternal flesh in order to overcome what none of us merely fleshly people could defeat.

The primary point of the early chapters of 1 Corinthians is that any attempt to see a deeper wisdom than this, to find what is going on "behind" the cross, is its own undoing. Believing that one *can* fathom God is the surest way to never do so. Any attempt to outthink God is the definition of futility. Every effort to outwit Him only proves itself an utter lack of wit. Trying to understand God is proof that you do not.

"No human being might boast in the presence of **God**" (1 Corinthians 1:29, emphasis added), and this is for glorious reason. Our thoughts cannot compare with His. Our words have nothing to offer Him. True wisdom is to know that God's wisdom is beyond us.

The evil within our nature resists this creaturely limitation. But it's precisely this limitation that is the seedbed of the glory of God's *grace*.

It is only the God who can command your silence who has true power to speak. It is only the God who needs nothing from you who truly has the power to give.

Letter to the Corinthians, Chapters 1–3: Bodily Boasting

There is one body. (Ephesians 4:4)

PAUL DOES not merely say that "no human being" may boast in the presence of God. He speaks with far more spice than that. While for much of the epistle he will rely on the calm and slightly sterilized σῶμα, Paul kicks off his letter with a far more earthy, carnal, guttural word. A dark word. The kind you might shush your kid for saying out loud in public.

"Flesh."

Not only in English but especially in the Greek of his day, σάρξ (sarx) is an ultimately tactile, utterly physical, somewhat dirty word. Far removed from the hyper–politically correct, semisterilized vanilla flavor of the inclusive "human being," σάρξ often will act for Paul as a pet reference to the condition of original sinfulness. It is no accident that he uses it here.

"No flesh may boast in the presence of God" (1 Corinthians 1:29, author's translation).

First, he means no mere creature. Nothing so limited as to require a material form has any chance of comprehending the ultimate and eternally immaterial God. This almighty God **made** all such forms with the breath of His mouth. We are but dust on our best days. In a battle of words with Him, we are surely lost.

"*flesh*" **is a dirty word**

But with that much established, and even more so, how much less could any such creaturely dust peer into divine mysteries from the far side of wicked and chaotic self-corruption? We humans are no longer "mere" dust. We are *chaff*. We are *bent*. Even our reason and logic, at its very height and pinnacle, is the reason and logic of selfish, evil creatures who are willing to twist all things for our own individual benefits. From such a fallen position, the dregs of depravity, there is no possibility in heaven or earth for us to lay any claim on God.

Until now.

Because, on both levels, Jesus of Nazareth has changed all of this.

He saved the chaff. He bought humanity, becoming our "righteousness and sanctification and redemption" (1 Corinthians 1:30). In order to do this, He became one with us. In order to be that dead body hung on a tree, the Wisdom beyond all wisdom became Wisdom in the *flesh* (John 1:14).

Almighty, ultimate, immaterial God became a *body*. In an axis-shifting, world-colliding moment, late in time He *en*fleshed. He entered our σάρξ. Wisdom as creature. Wisdom as *sinner*. Sinner without personal sin. Perfect man with all the sins of the world.

almighty God became a creature

"The testimony of God" (1 Corinthians 2:1) was born of a virgin, with Adam's DNA flowing through His veins, all so that He could bring that DNA into the grave and then out again. But this one "human being" Jesus Christ did not stop with the resurrection of His body. With His now-purified human σάρξ, He was, for the first time, a human now worthy to boast in God's presence.

So that is exactly what He did.

He *ascended*, bringing His body with glorious triumph into the presence of God. There, before the Unbegotten, He declared what He had accomplished. Upon this boasting, the Ancient of Days did not frown but smiled, for here in this man was also the restoration of all things.

Son of God, having become a tactile, gray-mattered, enfleshed man, now owns the right to press His boasting back into space, time, and human history. *Into* us. Into *you*.

More than co-workers in a field. More than well-placed stones in a building. More than tightly knit joints and marrow. Our unity with Him means that we are "Christ's, and Christ is God's" (1 Corinthians 3:23).

This is the heart of Paul's concern for Corinth. No flesh may boast apart from Jesus. Apart from His one, singular body, there is no hope. There is no life. There is no restoration. Nothing we hold or possess or earn or achieve has any lasting value by itself. The only value that exists for mankind is the value that the physical, raised, ascended body of Jesus Christ is.

But the Corinthians were failing to "spiritually discern" this (see 1 Corinthians 2:14b); they were instead falling back into merely "natural" (1 Corinthians 2:14a) ways of thinking. The rest of life and worldly thinking teaches us to make distinctions among ourselves based on our successes,

nonessential distinctions vie to supplant needful truth

our preferences, and our viewpoints. The Corinthians, just like everyone else, were experts in focusing on such trivialities.

"Paul baptized me."

"Apollos preaches better."

"Peter is the chief of them all!"

Perhaps the one who plants must work harder than the one who "waters" (1 Corinthians 3:7), but such arguments are irrelevant to Paul. More than that, they are *dangerous*. They are sprouts of ἑτερο-διδαχή. At first, such divisions may not seem like much of a threat to the seeds of faith. But once full-grown, entrenched and fighting for the same soil, nonessential distinctions vie to supplant and cast aside the most needful truths from their essential places.

This is why Paul uses such aggressive language. He chides the Corinthians for their willing jeopardy. He tells them that they are "still of the flesh," σάρξ (1 Corinthians 3:3). "Merely human" (1 Corinthians 3:4). "Sold under sin" (Romans 7:14). ἑτερο-διδαχή always begins as a slow drift. But it cannot remain so for long. Soon, it must compel the authentic διδαχή to diminish.

Once that is allowed, once falsehood and human opinion take root as if they were eternal truth, it's only a matter of time until eternal truth is muffled, covered, chased away, and/or forgotten.

"Jesus Christ and [His body] crucified" (1 Corinthians 2:2) is the διδαχή. He is "the way, and the truth, and the life" (John 14:6). The loss of true διδαχή, the replacement of mind of God with human distinctions, the substitution of our opinions for His doctrine, is necessarily rejection of *Him*.

Letter to the Corinthians, Chapters 3–7: Against the Body

> But He was speaking about the temple of His body. (John 2:21)

TODAY, YOU are more likely to hear "Do you not know that you are God's temple?" (1 Corinthians 3:16) quoted as some bizarre proof-text about Christian dieting than about being a community of people who are united physically to Jesus Himself. But it's the latter that is Paul's driving point.

"Temple" is Old Testament talk for "the place where God lives." Saying that you are God's temple is the same thing as saying that "God's Spirit dwells within you" (1 Corinthians 3:16). While this might seem tame to the mystical edge of American Christianity, it is a truly *radical* idea.

No godly Hebrew would ever suggest that an average believer is also God's temple. This is not because they were mistaken. They were right! God had a temple. It was a building in a very specific location, chosen by God, in which sat a box on which God Himself was known to sit with some regularity in the form of a glowing cloud. But that was all *before* Jesus.

"Destroy this temple," Jesus said, speaking of His body, "and in three days I will raise it up."

He claimed it, and then He proved it by doing just as He said. When He was crucified, He refused to stay dead. This meant that for the first time ever, God's temple was no longer a building. God's temple was a human body. But this human body was still specific. He was still located. Walking next to you on the road, He was *Immanuel*, "God right here with us."

Jesus held this reality strictly within Himself by virtue of His being the eternal Son of God. No other human being has such a thing by our own rights or power. But any human being connected to the body of Jesus suddenly finds himself in a marvelous and unbelievable situation.

It is this virtue, this connection with the body of Jesus, that gives Paul the right to call Christians "God's temple." Yet even here, it is essential to notice the *plural*.

Unlike English, Greek does not use the word *you* for both individuals and groups. When we say, "Do you not know," we have to rely on the context of the sentence to help us understand whether we are talking to many people or one person. Not so for the Bible.

The old King James picked up on this: "Know ye not that ye are the temple of God . . . ?" Today, we would not be able to sound so cool. We'd need to say something eclectic like "y'all" or "you's guys." But that is no excuse for completely misunderstanding the verse!

There is no longer only "I" once "you" are in Jesus. Now there is only *we*. "There may be so-called gods in heaven or on earth . . . yet for us there is one God, the Father, . . . and one Lord, Jesus Christ, . . . through whom we exist" (1 Corinthians 8:5–6). This existence is because we are connected to Jesus. Then, *in* Jesus, we are also connected to all the Christians in the whole world.

It is on the basis of this that Paul begins to explain to the Corinthians why what you do with your body sexually matters not only to you but to the rest of us as well. Far less important than your nutrition, our unity in Jesus the διδαχή revolutionizes our view of sexuality. "The **body** is not meant for sexual immorality" (1 Corinthians 6:13, emphasis added).

Paul is not being arbitrary. This is no relic of patriarchal misogyny. "The body is not meant for sexual immorality, but **for the Lord**, and the Lord for the **body**" (1 Corinthians 6:13, emphasis added). "You" (plural, meaning every Christian in every time and place, i.e., "the Church") are physically unified to the human body of Jesus so much so that the actions you (individually) take with your body have a direct impact on *our* relationship with both you and Jesus together.

"You are not your own" (1 Corinthians 6:19). This is not symbolic talk. Our "bodies are members of Christ" (1 Corinthians 6:15) now in fact and in truth. To abuse your body is to abuse *our* body is to abuse *Him*.

"Shall I then take the members of Christ and make them members of a prostitute?" (1 Corinthians 6:15). No! So *real*, so *total* is the presence of Jesus in His unification with His Christians that if a Christian man sleeps with a prostitute, he compels Jesus—and in Jesus, the rest of us—to do so as well. This, therefore, is a greater evil than many others. Nearly all wicked things a man might do are done "outside the body, but the sexually immoral person sins against his own body" (1 Corinthians 6:18).

"A little leaven leavens the whole lump" (1 Corinthians 5:6). This is not merely a sin against yourself. It is a sin against us, and us together in Jesus.

In the same way, it's a marvelous two-way street for the gift of sexuality given to us in marriage. Within the confines of public and lifelong commitment, your unity with Jesus is even a benefit to your unbelieving spouse. "The unbelieving husband is made holy because of his wife, and the unbelieving wife is made holy because of her husband" (1 Corinthians 7:14). This does not mean that they are saved. But it *does* mean that in your connection to the body of Jesus, this specific, individual unbeliever is actually physically closer to God than other unbelievers. They may not be saved, but he or she is *in proximity* to salvation.

there is only "we" in Jesus

Once your body has been "washed . . . in the name of the Lord Jesus Christ" (1 Corinthians 6:11), you are more than a conduit. You are a physical extension of Him. You are not just His hands and feet in some paltry, limp-wristed mystical legalism. Your body is all of His body, and He is all of you. The same way that the DNA of your parents is the entirety of who you are created to be, your being tied to Jesus imputes to you everything of all that He is. You are not God by yourself, but you, plural, are His temple. He is with you. He is in you. "You are not your own" (1 Corinthians 6:19).

being bought with a price is a carnal shift

"So glorify God in your body" (1 Corinthians 6:20)!

Which one?

Your own hands and feet? The Church? Jesus Himself?

Yes. All of them.

Be "anxious about the things of the Lord, how to be holy in body" (1 Corinthians 7:34). Remember in all things that being "bought with a price" (1 Corinthians 6:20) is not some fine, fancy theory about spiritual floatiness. It is a carnal shift, an *in*carnational transubstantiation, a *real* presence of Jesus. This is not ideology. He is "in" you, *as* you, and you are a full-fledged member of the plural new humanity that is born again in Him.

Letter to the Corinthians, Chapters 8–10: Now Concerning Food

> Why, as if you were still alive in the world, do you submit to regulations . . . (referring to things that all perish as they are used) . . . ? (Colossians 2:20, 22).

WHATEVER else you and I might do as Christians, we ultimately do it as members of the body of Jesus. For many corners of life, this does not have evident consequences. When it comes to simple dieting, spiritually *we* "*are no worse off if we do not eat*" and *we* are "*no better off if we do*" (1 Corinthians 8:8, emphasis added).

This is not to deny that some foods are inherently unhealthy for you. It is to say that not every decision has moral implications. Some things can be *bad* for you without being *wrong*. Over many years too much sugar might swell you like a balloon and give you diabetes. Surely, this increases the odds of your untimely death, thus stealing you from both your family and your local congregation. But it will not steal faith in Jesus Christ from either you or from us. By themselves, non-moral choices "will not commend us to God" (1 Corinthians 8:8).

The tricky part is that in a world of "many 'gods' and many 'lords'" (1 Corinthians 8:5), even a simple meal can, at times, have much more going on than merely the food. This is especially true when the food impacts another Christian on "the ground of conscience" (1 Corinthians 10:25).

Conscience is the organ of faith. Whenever the conscience is involved, Christianity is involved. You may not be able to point to the conscience the way that you can point to your heart or your liver, but it's there. When conscience accuses you, the pangs you feel are as physical as any other experience that you have. For this reason, even though food offered to idols isn't "anything" (1 Corinthians 10:19), if a recent convert to Christianity believes that it is, especially because he knows all too well that "what pagans sacrifice they offer to demons" (1 Corinthians 10:20), then indeed that food has become something more than mere food.

"Not all things build up" (1 Corinthians 10:23) our trust in Christ. Even good and lawful things harm us when they distract us from the certainty of the διδαχή. Food offered to demons, by itself, cannot have a direct effect upon your faith. But this changes the moment you believe that it does. The moment you believe that it does, it already has! Nonessential things, treated as though they are essential, have *already* weakened your actual faith (sometimes precisely by convincing you that you are stronger). In that case, firmer trust in ἑτερο-διδαχή directly eclipses faith in διδαχή.

The people in Corinth were soul-deep in this problem, to such an extent that Paul was genuinely fearful that he might lose them altogether.

"Do not . . . be unaware," he says, that "our fathers . . . all passed through the [Red Sea], and . . . were baptized into Moses in the cloud and in the sea. . . . All ate the same spiritual food, and all drank the same spiritual drink. For they drank from . . . **Christ**. Nevertheless, with most of them God was not pleased, for they were overthrown in the wilderness." (1 Corinthians 10:2–5, emphasis added)

THIS IS A truly stunning set of assertions across the board. But its primary force is that of a warning. "These things took place as examples for us, that we might not desire evil as they did" (1 Corinthians 10:6). Because of the threat to the conscience, ἑτερο-διδαχή, even about something so small as a meal, is not just some minor mistake or difference of opinion. It is truly evil, and as evil it is destructive to the community of the faithful.

"Let anyone who thinks that he stands take heed lest he fall" (1 Corinthians 10:12), not only for his own sake but also for the sake of the entire congregation, for the plural *you*. Weak faith is to be tolerated but never encouraged. We are to bear each other's burdens, but we are not to believe each other's doubts. We are to participate in each other's struggles, but we are to do so because we already participate in Someone who is greater than them all.

Letter to the Corinthians, Chapter 10: Crossroads "Upon the Standing of Words"

> Far be it from You, Lord! This shall never happen . . . ! (Matthew 16:22)

THESE THINGS "were written down for our instruction" (1 Corinthians 10:11), he says. They are a warning. But along with that warning, St. Paul has turned a rather dynamic corner, one that he will not reverse from until all his body talk has reached a mind-boggling fulfillment.

No self-respecting modern Bible reader would ever dare to make the claims he makes. "Baptized into Moses"? "The Spiritual Rock which followed them . . . **was** Christ"? They "**drank** from" Him? Where is any of that in the text of Exodus? *Nowhere*, that's where.

But here *you* face a moment of supreme decision: What do you believe about the *source* of Paul's words?

I do not mean to seem trite. I mean to beg the question. *How does Paul know what he is talking about?*

Is this the normal conclusion of a man long at study in the Old Testament, reliant on those ancient texts alone to explain themselves? Or is this something more? Is this something *new*? Is Paul adding on a deeper insight given to the ancient words by the revelation of the new temple, who is the body of the one man Jesus Christ?

Asked another way, was this interpretation, or is this *revelation*? Is this statement merely *human*? Or is it also the infallible *Word of God*?

Most Christians regularly and gladly give voice to the confession that the Word of God as written in Scripture is both inspired and without error. But now that confession must be put to the test. The statement that "the Rock [at Horeb, struck by the staff of Moses] **was** Christ" (1 Corinthians 10:4, emphasis added) is an intersection of truths and a crossroads of faith. It is a test that will expose not only whether you believe God revealed some words to us but what limitations you will let your reason put upon those words.

On the surface, Paul certainly *seems* to be saying that the man we now call "Jesus," the guy who died on the cross, who rose out of our sins, not only visited the people of Israel in the wilderness during the days of the old covenant but did so *as a rock*. A big one. That this rock was also able to lead the people as a cloud and fire does not remove the impossible *substance* of Paul's statement. He doesn't say, "the Son of God" or "the angel of the Lord." He says, "*Christ*," a clear reference to the anointed son of David, a term that finds its full expression in the Baptism of Jesus of Nazareth in the Jordan River in order to fulfill all righteousness. This man, as a rock, had His side split in two, and from Him fresh water bled onto the earth in order that the people might drink of it. More than this, when they drank of it, according to the plain sense of Paul's words, they also drank from *Him*.

Coming to terms with the fact that Paul's words *must* be true does not solve all of our problems. The test drives even deeper when our minds inevitably move from *what* to *how*. How was "the Rock . . . Christ"? What kind of presence did He have? The words are straightforward, but that won't stop our modern minds, quagmired in skepticism, from seeking a way around them. There is no question that it's significantly easier to believe that Christ was present symbolically, or as a metaphor, than to believe that He was present in some trans-cosmic, tactile, fleshy way.

what limitations will you put on God's revelation?

But once we take this route, our own skepticism can't help but eventually undermine us. If Christ is only there symbolically, then He wasn't **actually** there. If He is only there spiritually, then the rock itself was most definitely **not** Christ. This not only then calls into question the single statement by Paul but the entire reality of his ability to deliver to us viable new revelations. Because the writing of St. Paul **is** new revelation, it is all the more irregular for him to assert that "Christ was there" in order to convince us that "Christ was **not** there." If what Paul says is sometimes the opposite of what he actually means, then how are we to determine which words from Paul are new revelations to be trusted, and which are not? At that point, the idea that the revelation is given to reveal anything substantial at all becomes nearly nonsensical in itself.

This is important because it taxes our **epistemology**. *Epistemology* is a fifty-cent word that sounds like something horrible your doctor needs to take care of every decade after you turn forty. But it's not, and it's an incredibly valuable idea. Rooted in three Greek words (ερι-ἵστημι-λόγος, epi-histami-logos), it's a virtual sentence in a single word. Literally, we might render it "the study of your own understanding." Practically, it's the question, how do I know that I know what I know? It is in this question that all crossroads of faith and understanding intersect.

What we do next will determine a myriad of further steps with regard to the kind of God we are willing to believe that Jesus Christ is able to be. Is what I know something that I know because I understand it, or is what I know something I know because God makes it so, even when I do not understand it? Am I only able to know things that are beneath the powers of my mind, or is it possible to know things beyond the power of my mind when a mind greater than my own **reveals** these things to me?

new revelation taxes our epistemology

Is the true God the kind of God whose own being and doing are limited by what we mortal men might ask or imagine? Or are His thoughts beyond our thoughts and His ways beyond our ways? Is He merely magnificent, or is He, in fact, supernatural? Has the potter no right over the clay, to do with a lump what He will? How much more is this not true when the molder is not a mere mortal pressing his hands against some lump he has found but is instead a Creator God, authoring His own reality?

What is Jesus truly capable of? May He only do miracles that make sense to you? May He only reveal things you already know?

The end of the game is that if we are to consistently maintain that Paul is inspired, then we also must believe that the **substance** of the human Christ was also really and truly present in a drinkable manner some fourteen hundred years before His incarnation.

Letter to the Corinthians, Chapter 10: Crossroads of Reasonableness

Behold! I tell you a mystery. (1 Corinthians 15:51)

YOU DO NOT need to understand God in order believe Him when He speaks. The term *sacramentum* was coined by St. Augustine for just this reason. He was searching for a way to describe the incomprehensibility of Jesus' words regarding the Lord's Supper. He simply reached for a Latin term any man on the street would have understood as describing an inexpressible mystery. Little did he know that he was starting a trend that would last centuries. Unfortunately, due to a long history of abuse at the hands of medieval churches, the word *sacrament* has picked up significant baggage for many Christians. But when used with its original intent, we will find no better term for succinctly describing Christ's presence as the Rock of Horeb.

How was Jesus present? **Sacramentally**. That is, His presence is both **real** and yet also a **mystery**. He was there, in everything that He is but certainly in ways beyond our understanding. The people of Israel did not watch Moses strike a crucified man with his staff. But that is the promise that Paul tells us was true all the same. As is the case with any and every promise, we are now dealing with something more than mere reason. Reason may yet have a part to play, but it's no longer the master. Both promises and mysteries dwell in the realm of *faith alone*.

There is no other way to receive a promise than by believing it. When you receive a promise from a friend or an enemy, the question at the root is usually not whether the terms of the promise are possible but whether the one making the promise is trustworthy. At the crossroads of "how we know what we know" we must eventually decide why we believe **whom** we choose to believe.

Is the earth flat? Most of us would say, "No, silly." But why? Have you seen it? flown around it in a spaceship? One might point to pictures, but one might just as easily point to virtual reality and the ability to doctor images with computers to make the most unbelievable things look real. So we don't believe the earth is round because of our experience with it. Rather, we believe it because we trust those who have the experience themselves, who are also considered to be trustworthy.

So, St. Paul says that Christ was with His people as a rock. This is sacramental to us. It is a mystery. We cannot understand how it's possible any more than we can understand how the earth is round from our position standing on it on a sunny day. But only utter folly would refuse the possibility simply because the understanding is beyond us at the given moment. To claim that a thing is "untrue" simply because I don't at the moment have the faculty to understand is the definition of the fool. One can only learn what one knows one doesn't yet understand.

mysteries dwell in the realm of faith alone

Because this is true with mere human words and thoughts, how much more so must it be the case with the almighty God? We can add to this that creating faith alone is a primary objective of this God of ours. It is the restoration of trust in God's words, without proof, that God is all about in the religion of Christianity. It was trust that Adam lost when he considered God's words about the tree untrustworthy and in need of testing. It is trust that must be restored if we are ever to live at peace with God again.

In this way, for mankind to again believe that God is who He says He is, we are in desperate need of words from Him that are true but not readily believable. Faith alone cannot be created where reason is able to prove the fact. A promise from God that could be proven, achieved, or shown by us would require no trust at all. It would establish no faith, and it would continue to affirm our trust in ourselves rather than liberate us into the trustworthiness of God.

This is the business Paul is in. He is the proclaimer of the trustworthiness of Jesus. The proof is in the resurrection, an established impossible fact that altered the history of everything. From this foundation, Jesus has established His position as the giver of **assertions**. He is no philosopher delivering grandiose propositions for His students to consider, dissect, and eventually surpass. He is dictating facts that, before He speaks them, are beyond discerning. They are hidden. Unfathomable. Mystery.

being reasonable is admitting the limitations of Reason

So, Paul also insists that the same Israelites for whom Christ was the Rock, and all their children after them, would "eat the sacrifices [and thus be] participants in the altar" (1 Corinthians 10:18) at the tabernacle. How do we know this? Because Paul has said it, and Paul is the one sent by Jesus to say it to us. Reason here is our servant, not our master. Reason helps us sound out the letters and make sense of the words in the sentence. It illumines the path that leads to the revelation, helping us learn what is meant by words like "eat" and "sacrifices" and "altar." But after this, Reason stops and bows the knee at the sacramental. After this, Reason is reasonable and admits its own limitations, pointing to faith as an altogether greater gift. To trust God is eternally more useful than to understand Him.

Letter to the Corinthians,
Chapter 10: Crossroads of Participation

> Behold! I tell you a mystery.
> (1 Corinthians 15:51)

REASON TEACHES us the meaning of the words themselves, and thereby leads us to the place where faith receives a mystery. In the case of this most recent assertion from Paul, the mystery lies deepest in the word *participation*. It is not mysterious that the Israelites ate meat as part of their public religious rituals. The altar in their temple existed for this purpose, with priests doing the daily work of taking in animals for sacrifices and returning to the worshipers a portion for them to eat. But how this eating was a κοινωνία (koinonia [coin-oh-knee-ah]) is a bit more difficult to comprehend.

Κοινωνία means *"**commonality**."* It is originally a word for describing things of low or common value, though it has a wide variety of edges that various words in English can bring out. *Association, fellowship,* and *communion* all do it justice. But at its root, κοινωνία is a public unification so intimate that it fundamentally impacts reality itself. There is nothing held in common that is not shared, and yet there is nothing truly held in common that is not individually used. No "association" only appears to be true. A "fellowship" that is merely a symbol is no fellowship at all. A "common union" that is not an actual union held in common is a fraud.

The Israelites themselves had no more proof of their κοινωνία in the altar of their God than we do. To be sure, there was a giant cloud, and at times a fire floating in the sky above them. These apparitions were certainly Godlike! But the visible presence of a Godlike thing does not guarantee unseen effects of His promises. This still requires faith.

So, when the slave-people in Egypt solemnly slaughtered their lambs at sunset that one fateful night, painting the blood on their doorposts and then retiring to their homes to eat the animal in full, they had no proof, no reason to believe that the meal itself would create such a presence among them that the marauding angel of death would find them unkillable. Rather, they were faced with a moment of conviction. "How do we know what we know? Is this Moses guy trustworthy? Have the things he has said will come to pass in the past in turn come to pass?" Which is more believable: that the truth-teller will tell a lie, or that the unbelievable truth might prove itself true all the same?

Centuries later, those who kept the remembrance of Passover had even less to see. No one died overnight if they did not eat. The deep past of the original event could no more be tested than you can test the location of the earth in the solar system during broad daylight. Instead, they were compelled to rely on a promise. They were compelled to live by faith alone. The words declared that by eating and drinking this lamb yet again, they were tied by its flesh to the holy altar of their holy temple, named as such by a holy God who could no longer be seen hovering above it.

Were the words alone sufficient? Many did not believe so. Countless families of Israel did not consider the rites of the temple to be enough proximity to God to keep the feasts. Whole generations of Israel did not participate in the altar but sought out high places and witchcraft to tickle their itching passion for gods they could understand.

But their faithlessness never nullified the faithfulness of God. It is that notion that Paul is most concerned with preaching. He is on a collision course with its meaning for the Corinthians themselves. His point about the Israelites is only an example meant to demonstrate the sufficiency of his present claims. So far as he is concerned, God's use of food in miraculous, trans-cosmic ways is nothing new. The power of κοινωνία did not pass away with the old covenant altar, but it has been superseded by an even more stunning revelation: "The cup of blessing that we bless, is it not a **participation** in the blood of Christ? The bread that we break, is it not a [fellowship, association, communion, commonality with] the body of Christ?" (1 Corinthians 10:16, emphasis added).

they were tied by lamb's flesh to a holy God

Letter to the Corinthians, Chapters 11–15: More Than Alone

If all were a single member, where would the body be? (1 Corinthians 12:19)

IT HAS ALL been moving toward this point, and it's from this point that everything else Paul has to say in the remainder of the letter hinges. The body of the Lord Jesus, risen and ascended to highest heaven, has already been declared to be the same as the "you, plural" body of Christ of which each of us is a member in His Holy Church. We know this is because it is declared to us to be true. How this happens is a sacramental reality, a mystery of unification beyond our understanding. The only thing that remains is to believe that this mystery does not happen in a vacuum, but just as it did for the Israelites of old, in a real, present Meal.

"Because there is one bread, we who are many are one body, for we all partake of the one bread" (1 Corinthians 10:17). Here, in this food, we find Paul's reason why in "sinning against your brothers and wounding their conscience . . . you sin against Christ" (1 Corinthians 8:12). Here, in this cup that is shared, we find Paul's reason to "be steadfast, immovable, always abounding in the work of the Lord" (1 Corinthians 15:58). Here, in his participation, we find the source of his free and clear proclamation that "you are the body of Christ and individually members of it" (1 Corinthians 12:27).

> For I received from the Lord what I also delivered to you, that the Lord Jesus on the night when He was betrayed took bread, and when He had given thanks, He broke it, and said, "This is My body, which is for you. Do this in remembrance of Me." (1 Corinthians 11:23–24)

THERE IS a "still more excellent way" (1 Corinthians 12:31). There is the need to see genuine commitment to the good of all things as the path of true discipleship. But this patient and kind love that Paul will exhort us toward is not unconnected from the need to discipline the "body and keep it under control" (1 Corinthians 9:27). It is an extension of it. It is an outgrowth from the fact that we all "belong to the body" (1 Corinthians 12:15, 16) precisely because the Holy Meal asserts this fact to us.

This assertion is no more symbolic than the assertion that "Christ has been raised" (1 Corinthians 15:20). There is no symbolic resurrection. There is no symbolic eating and drinking. There is no symbolic body. These are all the same truth. "As by a man came death, by a man has come also the resurrection of the dead" (1 Corinthians 15:21).

In. His. Body.

As.

His.

Body.

"As in Adam all die, so also in Christ shall all be made alive" (1 Corinthians 15:22).

in this food we find Paul's reason

To attempt to have this faith without having this promise is to reject this faith. To attempt to have this promise without having the meal to which it is attached is to attempt to have your life without a body.

Literally.

Jesus' body is no symbol

Our common union with Jesus, the κοινωνία we share, is the physical fact that "in a moment, in the twinkling of an eye . . . this perishable body must put on the imperishable, and this mortal body must put on immortality" (1 Corinthians 15:52–53). The substance of you that is inherited from Adam, bits of DNA that broke off and formed and then broke off and formed again, always corrupt, always dying, a mortal body, is being replaced by a better body, a better substance, a blood with life in Him. This is no symbol. "As was the man of dust, so also are those who are of the dust," but "as is the man of heaven, so also are those who are of heaven" (1 Corinthians 15:48).

Who could insist that these are mere words? Who could insist that this promise is merely spiritual? The Last Day will not be a matter of personal experience or individual faith but a corporate, corporal extension of the resurrected man's flesh and blood as the purifying replacement of our own.

> Just as the body is one and has many members, and all the members of the body, though many, are one body, so it is with Christ. For in one Spirit we were all baptized into one body—Jews or Greeks, slaves or free—and all were made to drink of one Spirit. (1 Corinthians 12:12–13)

This language is anything but the gutless, Gnosticizing, antihuman "spirituality" of the modern age. Like the Israelites of old at Horeb, the *sacramental* mystery has come upon us as well. Unless Christ is not truly raised, then we have come face-to-face with something significantly more than a memory. More than a feeling. A religion that supersedes and transcends all created things with such omnipotence that He does not disdain our flesh but *joins* it.

God. With. Us.

The same.

Yesterday. Today. Forever.

Letter to the Corinthians,
Chapters 11 Visited Closely: Jesus in People Skin

It is the LORD's Passover. (Exodus 12:11)

THERE IS only one body of Jesus Christ, and He is not a metaphor. But sadly, this is what the majority of evangelical Protestants have come to believe about His body. We have assumed into Jesus a hyper-spiritualizing that all but denies His incarnation. We've taken to using the phrase "body of Christ" to mean anything and everything except for His actual body. We speak of the Church's unity in merely social or symbolic terms. As a result, it's become all too common to also speak of our being the hands and feet of Jesus as if He doesn't actually have any, as if without us, He would have no body at all.

As radical as this plight is, it should not be a surprise. The hyper-spiritualizing of Jesus was set in motion long ago when, in the early years of the Reformation, some of its leading men could not come to terms on the text of 1 Corinthians 11. At the time, the disagreement appeared to be surface level, a very small thing, a 1 percent shift in understanding and focus. But as any graphing calculator will show you, a 1 percent angle, over time, creates an infinite drift away from the foundation.

It began as a small adjustment to the meaning of the word *is*, but it has since become a complete negation of the entire meaning of the paragraph. From there, however many centuries it took, the trajectory was set for a day when biblical scholars felt free enough to question the rest of Paul's assertions.

Not too long after 1517, for the first time in the history of Christianity, "This [bread] is My body" was taken to mean "This [bread] is *not* My body." By the heyday of Pietism in the 1700s, the habit of weekly Communion was so damaged by the novel assertion that communing too frequently robs it of meaning that, ever since, Jesus' description of "do this" with the word "often" may as well not have existed. The wine has not been wine since 1869, when Thomas Bramwell Welch invented pasteurization. An ordained Wesleyan clergyman and dentist considered it temperate to remove alcohol from Christianity's central ritual. In 1891, the cup ceased to be *"the* cup" when Rev. H. Webb of Scovill Avenue Methodist Church of Cleveland,

Ohio, introduced individual cups to his congregation on the well-meant but scientifically flawed assumption that it would provide better hygiene.[2] Much more recent but no less significant, the phenomena of celiac disease, gluten intolerances, and wheat allergies have introduced gluten-free options to the Holy Table, failing to notice that in the history of the world, no civilization before our own would dream of distributing baked-potato paste to people and calling it "bread." But what matter is that in a Christianity that openly tolerates scholars who don't even believe the plain words of Paul, "For I received from the Lord what I also delivered to you" (1 Corinthians 11:23), as they freely scoff at the idea that any of the New Testament documents were written in the first century?

The "for you" on which Dr. Luther, that great reformer, set so much of his own personal hope in salvation has without question been removed from the majority of devotional practice. The newness of the "new testament " can hardly be much believed by Christians who mandate that the Sabbath must be kept on Saturday, who insist that New Testament Christians obey Old Testament food restrictions, and who claim the shofar is a divinely ordained instrument of worship. Even more readily ignored are the nearly mad statements of Paul that "anyone who eats and drinks without discerning the body eats and drinks judgment on himself" (1 Corinthians 11:29), and that a congregation's misuse of the Supper is "why many of you are weak and ill, and some have died" (1 Corinthians 11:30). How can a modern Christian consider such Bible verses to be anything more than utter nonsense?

"As often as you eat this bread and drink the cup, you proclaim the Lord's death until He comes" (1 Corinthians 11:26). If this is truly so, then how in heaven's name do we ever arrive at a point in Christianity where the Lord's Supper is not the lynchpin of all evangelical efforts! Perhaps it's because we have also come to believe that His return is yet another metaphor. One can hardly deny that the resurrection of the body on the Last Day is one of the great lost doctrines of **such Bible verses must be utter nonsense**

---

2   Without question, the most sterilized item you will ever come into contact with at church will be a gold-plated cup filled with alcohol. The passing of the peace, shaking hands at the door, and passing out of the bread while also giving blessings upon people's hair and foreheads are far more likely means of spreading germs.

all Protestant confessions. But what does it even matter? More than a few churches are comfortable preaching the "gospel" of a "God without wrath who brought men without sin into a kingdom without judgment through the ministrations of a Christ without a cross."[3] In the end, one must ask, what in hell's deepest scheming actually is this *"remembrance"* that we think we have?

"If we judged ourselves truly, we would not be judged. But when we are judged by the Lord, we are disciplined so that we may not be condemned along with the world" (1 Corinthians 11:31–32). What do these words even mean to us now? "Let a person examine himself, then, and so eat of the bread and drink of the cup" (1 Corinthians 11:28). What must he examine? How does a person unworthily partake of a symbol? Can eating and drinking a metaphor possibly kill you?

Perhaps the examination itself is meant to be allegorical? At what point should not even our physical "eating and drinking" be called into question? How can this dead ritual of repetition not be a complete misunderstanding of Christ's intention as He told a final parable on the night He was betrayed? Would not the true spiritual feasting on Christ be better expressed through the practice of foot washing? Of course, the Quakers have beaten us to that punch, but only by setting a more ambitious pace down the slippery slope of adjusting the meaning of the word *is*. But against their position, the text of Scripture remains in all its stark plainness:

can eating and drinking a metaphor possibly kill you?

---

3   *The Kingdom of God in America,* New York: Harper & Row, 1959 [1937], p. 193.

> [Whoever] eats . . . in an unworthy manner will be guilty concerning the **body and blood** of the Lord. Let a person examine himself, then, and so eat. . . . For anyone who eats . . . without discerning **the body** eats . . . judgment on himself" (1 Corinthians 11:27–29, emphasis added), because "the Lord Jesus on the night when He was betrayed took bread, and when He had given thanks, He broke it, and said, 'This is My body, which is for you.'" (1 Corinthians 11:23–24)

So if the word *body* here is only a reference to all the Christians who make up Christ's Church on earth, then that means "Christ's body" and "Jesus' body" are two completely different things! Jesus is less than a member of Himself. He is an appendage, an appendix, something ***other than*** Himself.

If these words are only spiritual, then Christ is only spiritual. Any presence of Jesus without His body is the presence of a Christ who "has not been raised" (1 Corinthians 15:14, 17). Now He is more impotent than a God without wrath. He is more useless than a Kingdom without judgment. He is less than a Christ without a cross. He is a Word without flesh.

In such a case, Paul's warning to Corinth is well taken as a warning to us: "It is not the Lord's Supper that you eat" (1 Corinthians 11:20). 🐝

What Did John Touch?

No obscurity in the words Jesus spoke at the institution of the Supper is therefore responsible for the deeply regrettable eucharistic controversies, but only the assumption that he could not have meant what is expressed in the Words of Institution because these words as they stand assert something *impossible*.

Hermann Sasse

Therefore, in order that we may become of His Body, not in desire only, but also in very fact, let us become commingled with that Body. This, in truth, takes place by means of the food which He has given us as a gift, because He desired to prove the love which He has for us. It is for this reason that He has shared Himself with us and brought His body down to our level, namely, that, we might be one with Him as the body is joined with the Head. . . . And to show the love He has for us He has made it possible for those who desire, not merely to look upon Him, but even to touch Him and consume Him. . . . in short to fulfill their love.

John, the Golden Mouth

And the angel of the LORD appeared to him in a flame of fire out of the midst of a bush. He looked, and behold, the bush was burning, yet it was not consumed.

The Bible

The Good News of John: Material Oneness

Avoid the irreverent babble and contradictions of what is falsely called "knowledge." (1 Timothy 6:20)

THE FIRST chapter of John's Gospel is a full-throttle attack against the hyper-spiritualizing of Christianity in his day, which we would later come to know as Gnosticism. Rooted in the preaching of a secret "knowledge" (γνῶσις, or "gnosis"), Gnosticism was a powerful movement that cut straight to the heart of the physicality of Jesus. Over the centuries it took on various forms, but at its deepest root always lay the denial of one all-important fact: the body of Jesus is the body of God.

There were many ways to get around this truth. One might say that the one we know as Jesus was indeed God, but He only *appeared* to be or *seemed* to be a man. Or you could invert the equation and assert that the true God only *adopted* the body of Jesus for a time, but God certainly did not die with Him on the cross. Later teachers of ἕτερο-διδαχή (ἕτερο [hetero]-διδαχή [di-da-kay] or "different doctrine") would get even more creative, affirming the right words while also teaching that the body of Jesus and Godhood of Jesus never really joined together any more than two boards you might glue side by side.

In every case, the unifying factor for these false teachings was a discomfort with the physical assertions about God. The existence of God was not a problem, nor was the ability of God to manifest Himself in some way in order to teach us. It is that He might actually become one of us that caused a stir. It was the idea that the infinite God might limit Himself to a finite body that caused a stir.

Writing some sixty years or more after the other apostles, with most of them murdered in gruesome martyrs' deaths, John, the apostle "whom Jesus loved," wasted no time in attacking the issue head-on, insisting that the source of all γνῶσις is that the **Word** "became flesh and dwelt among us" (John 1:14). This Word he speaks of is far more than an idea, or notion, or even some eternal principle or spirit. This "Word was with God, and the Word was God" (John 1:1). Yet while the Word in John's Gospel rightly receives much attention, the book is utterly dripping with three other most important images: water, Spirit, and blood.

John is utterly dripping with water and blood

"This is He who came by water and blood," John writes in 1 John 5:6, "not by the water only but by the water and the blood. And the Spirit is the one who testifies." Most readers of the Bible won't find these words until many, many chapters after they have read about water and blood flowing from the pierced side of the crucified Jesus in John 19, but that is an unhappy chance of history and the organization of the biblical books. When taken together, John's Gospel and his letters form a tight unit, with each serving to explain the other.

It is no coincidence that the entire Gospel is centered on a movement from water to blood to Spirit, all culminating in those few fateful moments at Golgotha. This is John's design by intention. It is a driving point to highlight the tight unity of the substantial physicality of Jesus and the working of the Holy Spirit among His Church. "That which was from the beginning, which we have heard, which we have seen with our eyes, which we looked upon and have touched with our hands . . . was made manifest, and we have seen it, and testify to it" (1 John 1:1–2). For John, the true γνῶσις (knowledge) is one and the same as the διδαχή (*doctrine*), and **He** is no one other than Jesus Himself. This Jesus whom "we have seen and heard we proclaim also to you, so that you too may have fellowship [κοινωνία—"association," "communion"] with us; and indeed our fellowship [κοινωνία—"association," "communion"] is with the Father and with His Son Jesus Christ" (1 John 1:3).

"No one comes to the Father except through" Jesus (John 14:6). Union with Jesus is union with God, and the Spirit's work to testify about this gift to the world does not come without the body of Christ. "For there are three that testify: the Spirit and the water and the blood; and these three agree" (1 John 5:7–8). It is only the Gnostic, anti-material mind, both ancient and modern, that would create a division between them. John does not record Jesus preaching a division between human nature and the divine but a unity. "You, Father, are in Me, and I in You, that they also may be in Us . . . that they may be one even as We are one, I in them and You in Me" (John 17:21–23).

This is not to say that all mankind are to become gods. It is to emphasize the opposite: that God has become a new kind of man with the intent of raising up from the grave a new kind of humanity.

Three Who Testify

> He took the blood of calves and goats, with water
> and scarlet wool and hyssop, and sprinkled both
> the book itself and all the people. (Hebrews 9:19)

IT IS WATER that John baptizes with at Bethany, across the Jordan. He came baptizing with water in order that it might be revealed to Israel that among them stood One who is mightier than us all, One who could do much more than simply wash people with a demonstration of repentance, but who is capable of washing us "with the Holy Spirit" (John 1:33).

It is water that Jesus changes into wine on the third day at Cana. "Six stone water jars there for the Jewish rites of purification" (John 2:6) stand ready for use by a man who is not limited by the laws of our universe.

It is water that Jesus talks about when He is met in the dark of night by the rabbi Nicodemus. But the water is never alone. "Unless one is born of water and the Spirit, he cannot enter the kingdom of God" (John 3:5), He tells the confused teacher of Israel.

It is water that Jesus then instituted His disciples to baptize with "[in] the Judean countryside" (John 3:22), so much that it disturbed John's disciples. They cry out, "Look, He is baptizing, and all are going to Him" (John 3:26). But John replies that even this is a gift from heaven, filled with "words of God" and "the Spirit without measure" (John 3:34).

It is water that Jesus asks the woman of Samaria to draw forth from a well at the middle of the day. But receiving the water of the earth is not what He is after. Rather, He says, "If you knew the gift of God, and who it is that is saying to you, 'Give Me a drink,' you would have asked Him, and He would have given you living water" (John 4:10).

It is in the town of Cana, "where He had made the water wine" (John 4:46), that Jesus heals the official's son with but a word, demonstrating yet again that all things in heaven and on earth are subject to His command.

It is water that filled the "pool, in Aramaic called Bethesda," which had five roofed colonnades and stood by the Sheep Gate in Jerusalem, whereby "lay a multitude of invalids—blind, lame, and paralyzed" (John 5:2–3). Among them was a man who had lain there daily for thirty-eight years, hoping in the vain lie that the waters would be touched by angels and so bring him healing. Something far greater than an angel stood before him that day, as Jesus commanded him, "Get up, take up your bed, and walk" (John 5:8).

It is not water but food to which John turns next, having already seeded the connection between bread and Jesus with the disciples urging Jesus to eat. "I have food to eat that you do not know about" (John 4:32). The disciples think He is speaking of only ordinary things, but Jesus insists that His mind is set on a far greater harvest.

It is bread that Jesus multiplies on a barren hillside, where the fields were ripe with over five thousand people seeking to hear His words. He "took the loaves, and when He had given thanks, He distributed them" (John 6:11) in yet another demonstration that whatever limitations nature might have, in the human hands of Jesus those boundaries are shattered with miraculous possibility. In what reality does one wind up with more of a thing after it has been given away? Yet, "they gathered them up and filled twelve baskets with fragments from the five barley loaves left by those who had eaten" (John 6:13).

It is water that Jesus walks on that very night, while His disciples huddle terrified in their little boat. "Do not be afraid," He said, and "they were glad" (John 6:20, 21) to take Him into the boat, which immediately, and impossibly, defied physical reality and reached its intended destination.

It is bread that the crowds were after the next day, having traveled earnestly around the Sea of Tiberias to search out Jesus. Search for "the food that endures to eternal life" (John 6:27), Jesus chides them, much as He had the woman by the well: "The bread of God . . . who comes down from heaven and gives life to the world" (John 6:33).

It is bread that Jesus claims to be, stunning the crowds with His insistence that "whoever comes to Me shall not hunger, and whoever believes in Me shall never thirst" (John 6:35). But now He is truly going too far. Now He is asking too much to be believed, and a great debate ignites over the power of Jesus to do what He says. The skeptics "grumbled about Him, because He said, 'I am the bread'" (John 6:41).

It is flesh that Jesus insists they eat, and it is blood that He demands they drink, if

Jesus' hands shatter nature with miraculous possibility

they have any hope of being raised up to eternal life on the Last Day. This is not any old flesh, nor any old blood, but that which is given to them in Himself, the Son of Man. "Whoever feeds on My flesh and drinks My blood abides in Me, and I in him" (John 6:56).

It is the Spirit whom the people reject when they complain, "This is a hard saying; who can listen to it?" (John 6:60). It is the Spirit who is offensive in His demands that human flesh alone is worthless, that human minds alone are limited, that human expectations are too narrow and too vain. "The words that I have spoken to you are spirit and life. But there are some of you who do not believe" (John 6:63–64).

It is bread and blood, of "fine flour mixed with oil" (Numbers 7:13), from bulls, rams, lambs, and goats, which all the people, Jesus included, celebrated in the offerings and sacrifices of the eight days of the Feast of Booths when He "went up, not publicly but in private" (John 7:10). It is water that intertestamental tradition had caused to be carried from the Pool of Siloam with great ceremony, all the way to the temple courts, where the priests carried it around the altar while chanting the great Hallel of Psalms 113–118. But it is on the last day of the feast, the eighth day, the great day, when the water libations reach their climax as the priests circle the altar seven times shouting, "Hosanna!" that Jesus "stood up and cried out, 'If anyone thirsts, let him come to Me and drink. Whoever believes in Me, as the Scripture has said, "Out of His heart will flow rivers of living water"'" (John 7:37–38).

It is water that filled the same Pool of Siloam that Jesus passed by on His way down from the temple, where Jesus "saw a man blind from birth" (John 9:1).

It is water that Jesus spit from His mouth and mingled with the earth in order to make mud that He packed upon the man's eyes.

It is water from both Siloam and Jesus' mouth that the man washed over his face at Jesus' command, and having "washed [he] came back seeing" (John 9:7).

It is water that filled the Jordan River, where Jesus retired after His Spirit was rejected by the leadership during that tumultuous week, and where He remained until His friend Lazarus died.

It is water that flowed down His cheeks when "Jesus wept" (John 11:35), standing by the tomb of His friend, for He loved him much.

It is flesh and blood, living by the power of the Spirit, who walked out of the tomb at Jesus' beckoning, against all reason and strength stripped of his odor and decay. "Did I not tell you that if you believed you would see the glory of God?" (John 11:40).

It is blood that would be spilled by lambs for each household at the Feast of Passover, for which Mary christened our Lord's feet with nard as a proclamation of His impending burial. Large crowds who had gathered for that feast, filled with the eating of unleavened bread, hurried to line the streets as He entered the city.

it is bread and blood Jesus celebrated

It is water that Jesus took in a bowl and used to wash His disciples' feet before they ate that bread together. Peter, still blinded by his nature, declared, "You shall never wash my feet." But the water Jesus brought was of utmost necessity: "If I do not wash you, you have no share with Me" (John 13:8).

It is bread that Jesus took after supper and gave to His disciples with marvelous words, though John does not recall it. Rather, it is the bread that He gave to Judas, while John leaned against His chest, which John recalls. After Iscariot had taken that morsel in unbelief, "Satan entered into him," and Jesus said, "What you are going to do, do quickly" (John 13:27).

It is the Spirit whom Jesus preached after the betrayer had left: "the Spirit of truth, whom the world cannot receive" (John 14:17). Four solid chapters of Jesus' teaching and prayer hover over the central truth that the Spirit of God, when He comes, however He comes, "will bear witness about Me" (John 15:26). He will bear witness about Jesus. "He will guide you into all the truth, for He will not speak on His own authority, but whatever He hears He will speak" (John 16:13). He will take what is Christ's and declare it to the world. The Spirit will call to mind the words the Father gave to Jesus— and Jesus gave to His apostles—that we might be sanctified in His truth.

It is the Spirit who makes us believe that Christ is in us, and the Father is in Christ; that we are all perfectly one. Through these words we are all made one, we in God and God in us, "that the love with which" (John 17:26) the Father loved His Son might also be in us, and Christ in us.

Then there is silence. Then there is nothing. There is neither Spirit nor water nor blood.

There were men out for blood who came armed with torches to take Jesus away, and there was blood shed by Peter when he struck the ear of Malchus. But none of this is mentioned by John.

Jesus was struck. Peter fled in despair. We know that Pilate washed his hands, but water, blood, and Spirit remain silent.

They take Jesus out, bearing His cross. What is written, is written. But it's only near the end, when jars filled with sour wine have replaced those from the wedding at Cana, that Jesus, knowing that all was now finished, said in the Spirit, "I thirst" (John 19:28). "He bowed His head and gave up His Spirit" (John 19:30).

Only then, that three might testify and three might agree, do the soldiers come, intent on breaking His legs. But finding Him already dead, they instead pierce His swollen, asphyxiated heart, a final testimony to the world. "At once there came out blood and water. He who saw it has borne witness—his testimony is true, and he knows that he is telling the truth—that you also may believe" (John 19:34–35).

It is the Spirit Jesus gives on the day of resurrection, when He showed them His hands and His side from which the blood and water had flowed. "He breathed on them and said to them, 'Receive'" (John 20:22).

It is water that Peter and Thomas, Nathanael, and the sons of Zebedee were fishing on the whole night long, catching nothing, when they saw Jesus on the shore, shouting, "Cast the net on the right side of the boat" (John 21:6).

It is food that they found on the shore, after Peter had been washed, head to toe, in his haste to get to Jesus.

It is bread that Jesus took and "gave it to them" (John 21:13) to eat with the fish before He asked them of their love and commanded them to feed the world with His words.

It is "the supper" (John 21:20) that John mentions when describing himself as the one who bears witness about these things.

What does any of this mean? It means next to nothing, for none of it directly speaks of baptismal regeneration nor the eating of the body and blood of Jesus as the bread and wine of Holy Communion. Except that it means everything, for only willful blindness can ignore John's constant, even toying, reference to the material elements of Christianity's most ancient rituals. Only the most obstinate of skeptics can think that any of this is an accident. Only a crass fool refuses to believe the Spirit's work among the children of fallen man by resisting the plainness of Jesus' words with the question, "What is truth?" (John 18:38). Faith sees that the Spirit makes believing men by awakening them to the wisdom given in the plainly unbelievable words of Jesus.

"I Am" *Is Not* "Is Not"

> God said to Moses, "I AM WHO I AM." And
> He said, "Say this to the people of Israel:
> 'I AM has sent me to you.'" (Exodus 3:14)

FOR ALL that St. John does to point us to the testimony of the Spirit by means of water and blood, he is also a favorite source of proofs against a straightforward reading of "This is My body." For many modern Bible readers, jumping from author to author and putting a great deal of faith in unbiased translations has led to a use of Jesus' many "I am" statements throughout John as "proof" that Jesus often spoke figuratively, with the result that we should take His "This is" statements with the same understanding we would apply to His "I am's."

The great danger of this approach is its foundational assumption that Jesus doesn't really mean it when He says "I am." It turns out that in order to maintain the position that "This is" means "This is not," it's stunning what we are willing to assume Jesus is not, even though He says clearly, "I am."

Jesus makes at least seven obvious "I am" statements in John. He says, "*I am . . .*

"the bread of life" (John 6:35, 48);

"the light of the world" (John 8:12; 9:5);

"the door of the sheep" (John 10:7, 9);

"the good shepherd" (John 10:11, 14);

"the resurrection and the life" (John 11:25);

"the way, and the truth, and the life" (John 14:6);

"the vine, and you are the branches" (John 15:5).

These seven statements stand out in the Greek more than they do in English thanks to another quirk of the languages. In Greek, there are two different ways to say "I am." The most common way is with the use of a single word, εἰμι (ae-me). This word has both of the English words *I* and *am* built into it. But there is a second, more emphatic turn of phrase, in which the speaker effectively uses the word *I* twice. A literal rendering of Ἐγώ εἰμι (ae-go ae-me) into English comes out terribly awkward: "I, I am." But for the native Greek speaker, it would have been heard more along the lines of "I really, really, really say that I am."

As a result of this unique emphasis by Jesus, the seven "I am" statements of John stand out from the many other places where Jesus says, "I am." Clearly, St. John wanted to drive home a point, which perhaps comes to bear the most in John 8:58, where Jesus once again says, "Before Abraham was, [I, I am]." At this point, those who were listening were so enraged by the saying that they took up rocks in their hands with the intention of beating Him to death with them. It might seem a bit extreme, but in their mind-set anyone who claimed to be eternal, or one with God, deserved such a fate. Blasphemy was a capital crime under Hebrew law, and Jesus was evidently committing it.

they took rocks with the intention of beating Him to death

Of course, as Christians we relish this moment as one in which Jesus confesses His divine nature before the world. He had already challenged the people to "Destroy this temple, and in three days I will raise it up" (John 2:19), which John then insists is a reference to His death and resurrection. Jesus' later claim to be more ancient and everlasting than Abraham fits directly into this central point of John's entire Gospel. But conflict arises when we start comparing the literal nature of these claims with the alleged symbolic nature of Jesus' other Ἐγώ εἰμι statements.

It is easiest to make the claim with Jesus' statements about being a door and a vine. This is usually as far as the argument ever goes.

"Jesus said, 'This is My body,' therefore the bread is His body."

"Yes, but Jesus also said, 'I am the vine,' and clearly Jesus is not a vine.

He speaks symbolically, and you would do well to understand that."

It is hard to argue back. None of us think that Jesus was a houseplant or a wooden object. That is just plain silly. But a problem arises if we do not stop there and look for consistency in the rest of the statements.

When Martha, the sister of Lazarus, meets Jesus outside her home and makes the marvelous confession, "Lord, if You had been here, my brother would not have died" (John 11:21), Jesus confronts her grief with the insistence that He Himself *is* the resurrection. What are we to do with the argument that at this point He is only speaking symbolically? Jesus then proceeds to raise Lazarus from the dead with only a word. But greater still, He goes forth to meet His own death in order to conquer, just as He prophesied. Not only does that epic event signify His physical embodiment of the ability to defeat death, but the entire hope of the Christian life is founded on the belief that His resurrection was not *only* His resurrection; it's also the resurrection of all who will come to believe in Him.

The other Ἐγώ εἰμι statements present similar conundrums. Is Jesus only figuratively the good shepherd? Surely Christians are not small wooly animals that need shearing, but neither do we need to be for Jesus to actually be the one who shepherds us as any good king would. What then of "the way, and the truth, and the life"? Does Jesus only represent these things? Anyone who would claim that Jesus is not really the light of the world will have great difficulty with the moment of His transfiguration, not to mention John's Revelation claim that the world to come "has no need of sun or moon to shine on it, for the glory of God gives it light, and its lamp is the Lamb" (Revelation 21:23).

As is always the case, the problem is not with Jesus' words but with our insistence that they be shoehorned into our previous assumptions. The original argument that Jesus is not an actual wooden door is a tremendously wooden and overly obtuse rejection of the language of the text. Jesus never says, "I am a wooden door." Jesus says, "I am *the* door." The difference between these two statements is astronomical. A door is only made of wood if it's a door to a house. But a door can also be many other things, such as a hole in the ground, an opening to new thought, or a wormhole-like portal to another dimension.

Jesus really means it: He is the only opening that exists for mankind to enter into eternity. This is literal, and it is substantiation in the highest order. His claim to be *the* vine is no different. He is the only root for humanity's resurrection. No other source of lifeblood exists that can take us from the valley of shadow to the city of the great King.

All down the line, Ἐγώ εἰμι shows itself to be a tremendously "not symbolic" statement. "Before Abraham was, I am [Ἐγώ εἰμι]" cannot possibly be symbolic without denying the incarnation of the Son of God.

Jesus never says, "I am a wooden door"

"[Ἐγώ εἰμι] the resurrection and the life" (John 11:25) cannot in any way be merely spiritual without denying Jesus' own resurrection from the dead. All the more so, "[Ἐγώ εἰμι] the bread of life" (John 6:35, 48) should be taken by modern Christians with all the earnest seriousness that the people at Capernaum took it. That they misunderstood it to mean that Jesus wanted people to eat His flesh and drink His blood without the use of bread and wine can only be blamed on their hardness of heart. "Lord, to whom shall we go?" (John 6:68) is the response of faith to all claims by Jesus that might defy our understanding.

Jesus *is* the light of the world, and He proved it when He glowed on top of a mountain.

Jesus *is* the doorway to eternal life, and He guarantees this with the promise that all who are baptized into His death are also baptized into His resurrection.

Jesus *is* the good shepherd, who, enthroned between the cherubim in the highest heaven, leads His people like a flock.

Jesus *is* the vine, and we are the branches. Apart from Him, we can do nothing but die. Without literal, tangible, human connection to Him, we are nothing but the decaying fruit of Adam's root.

Jesus *is* the way. No one comes to the Father except through His flesh and blood. Jesus *is* the truth. He is the eternal word who as flesh has dwelt among us. Jesus *is* the life, and that life is the light of men.

Jesus *is* the resurrection. For you. For me. For the life of the world.

Jesus *is* the bread, which when eaten, will raise you up on the Last Day.

His Ἐγώ εἰμι is not proof to the contrary. If anything, it's a more emphatic proof of the same thing that all the other Gospels, and Paul with them, have said all along.

A Participally Perfect Conclusion

If anyone loves Me, he will keep My word, and
My Father will love him, and We will come to
him and make Our home with him. (John 14:23)

THERE ARE two rules of thumb when seeking to understand the themes and focal points of Scripture. First, if something is mentioned often and everywhere, you can bet that it's fairly important. In this way, the resurrection of Jesus, the impending judgment of the world, and salvation for those who are in Christ are written with such constant confession that we would be fools to ignore their meaning.

On the other hand, there are other doctrines that are imperative not because they are spoken of so often but because when they are spoken of, their implication and meaning are so deeply central and world altering. Examples of this would be justification by grace alone, the original sinful condition of mankind, and, of course, the Lord's Supper.

we have touched the physicality of Christianity

There is a third category that is also important. These are those topics in Scripture that are only spoken about one time or in one limited context. These revelations can at times be confusing or unclear. Without other verses to compare them with, we cannot easily apply the practice of Scripture interpreting Scripture. Such topics include marriage in the afterlife, the order of Melchizedek, and how the angels feel about our hair length.

In every case, if we hunger for the truth, we should seek every possible verse that illuminates the meaning of the others, building our trust on the clarity of what we find. When this is done with the Lord's Supper, when Scripture alone is allowed to understand itself, it becomes increasingly difficult to logically accept the skeptic's view of the bodily presence of Jesus in sacramental ways, allowing Christians in the present to eat His flesh and drink His blood in the forms of bread and wine.

The Gospels of Matthew, Mark, and Luke all speak exactly the same way. Though each adds or removes various elements of Jesus' Words of Institution, they never tinker with the central statement "This is My body," even though the Greek presented them every opportunity to do so. St. Paul confirms their confession, passing on to us what he received directly from Jesus Himself in the exact same words, while adding an insistence that there is a mysterious κοινωνία ("association," "communion") at work in the meal itself. Decades later, with all the other apostles dead, St. John pushes full-throttle forward with brash statements about eating flesh and blood that is real food and real drink, while making the unity between the Spirit of God and the blood of Jesus a driving theme of his entire Gospel.

But St. John didn't stop there. Although they are at times forgotten books of the New Testament, John also wrote three letters to the churches under his care. It is in the first of these letters that we find his marvelous statement "three that testify: the Spirit and the water and the blood; and these three agree" (1 John 5:7–8). But this does not come to us in a vacuum. It is a major concluding comment in a long work emphasizing the physicality of Christianity. It is what "[we] have touched with our hands, concerning the word of life" (1 John 1:1) that John proclaims to us "so that you too may have [κοινωνία] with us; and indeed our [κοινωνία] is with the Father and with His Son" (1 John 1:3–4). While these verses do not speak openly about drinking the blood of Jesus, the entire letter gravitates around the necessity of His blood for us. "If we walk in the light, as He is in the light, we have [κοινωνία] with one another, and the blood of Jesus His Son cleanses us from all sin" (1 John 1:7).

What does it mean to walk in the light? What is the commandment that John insists we have had from the beginning, that we must keep? What is the testimony of God that is greater than man's testimony? How is it that we can be certain we have overcome the evil one? When the spirit of the antichrist teaches men to deny Jesus, what will he teach falsely about Him? If we wish to abide in Christ, how should we do so?

All of this comes to a head when John says,

> Beloved, do not believe every spirit . . . for many false prophets have gone out into the world. By this you know the Spirit of God: every spirit that confesses that Jesus Christ has come in the flesh is from God, and every spirit that does not confess Jesus is not from God. This is the spirit of the antichrist, which you heard was coming and now is in the world already. (1 John 4:1–3)

A whole book could be written on the meaning of "antichrist" as a biblical term and how vastly divergent it is from the way we normally use the word. For John, it's clearly not an end times persona so much as a spirit of lies that will teach things that are "anti" or "against" Christ's teaching. False preachers are warned of constantly in the New Testament, waterless springs who will go about teaching their own ideas as if they were the words of God. In order to guard against being deceived by them, John exhorts us to seek the Spirit of God in a particular confession: *that Jesus Christ has come in the flesh*" (1 John 4:2).

On the surface, this appears to focus our discernment on the incarnation of Jesus. Clearly, this has been a concern for John throughout his Gospel and it should not surprise us to see him combating the same ἑτερο-διδαχή here. The threat of a religious movement called Gnosticism was real and present for him and the Christians of his day. (Gnosticism, named for its emphasis on enlightening "secret

Gnosticism preached a devaluation of the body

knowledge," preached the principles of Platonic philosophy, especially the devaluation of material things like human bodies, muddled within the pantheons of Greek mystery cults dressed up in the style of Christianity.) But what may appear simple on the surface in English can often have much deeper consequences for original language speakers.

It is not as though the translation is incorrect. The challenge is that the particular turn of phrase John uses here in 1 John 4:2, and later again in 2 John 7, is something that we simply cannot translate into English. More than risking a wooden sound such as the "I, I am" of Ἐγώ εἰμι, we simply have no equivalent.

If you really, really hate grammar with a passion, then please feel free to skip ahead a few paragraphs, as we're about to get geek-deep into it. But if we care about the meaning of the Scriptures, then at times like this we have little other choice.

In English, we have three basic forms of conjugating verbs. That means that when we speak about actions, we can speak about those actions in three different ways: past, present, and future. We shift between these forms of speaking about doing without thinking twice about it. The difference between "he runs" and "he ran" is organic for us. We also have other less used and more peculiar conjugations, usually requiring more words. "He has run" and "having had run" allow us to impart more nuanced meaning to our sentences. It's this latter type of nuance that we are dealing with in 1 John 4:2. But it's even more peculiar than that.

Unlike English, Greek's basic forms of conjugation are not rooted in *time*. Why this might be is a subject for someone who loves the history of how English as a language came to be. As a language arising to dominance after the advent of the clock, it can't help but have been influenced in seeing time as a dominant form of life's meanings. The Greeks, while certainly aware of time, did not infuse their language with it. Rather, their conjugations were more concerned with **connection**.

That can be a pretty esoteric idea without some meat on it. But as an example, Greek does not truly have a "past" tense. It has a "completed" tense, which we nerds call the **aorist**. When a Greek said "he ran," he did not mean "at a former time, running happened" so much as "the running that so and so was doing is now completed." This might seem trivial until we run into the **second** way that Greeks could speak about the past, called the **imperfect**. When this form of word is used, "he ran" wouldn't be about the end of the running but the continuation or connection of the running to the rest of the event. We might say, "I was running when such and such happened" to convey a similar idea.

All of this is only to demonstrate how complex Greek verbs can be. Then things get tougher! Greek has another past tense called the **perfect**. It is quite rare by appearance when compared with the other two forms and has a strong focus on the **results** of the past action. While we also have a perfect tense in English, "He **had** run," the clear connection to results is not as evident as it is in Greek.

As if that wasn't nuanced enough, enter the **participle**. Participles generally exist in many languages to allow the speaker to use an action in connection with another action. "**Running**, he fell." But where for English speakers the participle is fairly wooden, always involving an "-ing" ending and part of a participial phrase, the participle in Greek is like a language unto itself. The participle can be used in multiple tenses, with aorist, imperfect, present, and future all containing different edges of meaning.

enter the participle

Then, you hit the jackpot. Every once in a while, every fifth or sixth blue moon, a Greek speaker will be so intense as to use a *perfect participle*. This is the form we've been working toward, the one John employs in 1 John 4:2 and 2 John 7. It is the form that we have no simple way to translate into English. Its purpose is to talk about both past and present at the same time, with the *results* of a past action being so permanent as to continue having an impact right now. The technical language is "a past event with a present enduring result."

Sticking with our running man, to accurately translate a Greek perfect participle we would have to say, "He ran in such a way that he is still running now." Running isn't the kind of thing that would normally require this manner of talking, which explains why the form is so rare. Even when we do find these little nuggets, most translations will usually pick a point of emphasis that seems prevalent and leave it at that. In other words, we would see the "perfect running" word in Greek and then translate it either as "he has run" or "he is still running," with the hope of conveying the largest portion of true meaning.

With this in mind, most translations of 1 John 4:2 state that "Jesus Christ has come in the flesh" because they believe the emphasis of the verse is on the past action of Christ to incarnate among us. But what is lost in translation is that there is a present, enduring, ongoing coming in the flesh that Jesus continues to do.

It is understandable that translations done by Christians who do not believe in the sacramental presence of Christ in the Supper might miss this important edge. By training, they are not looking for it. But it's right there, clear as purple crayon, in the original manuscript. "Jesus Christ has come [in the past with such an effect that He is still coming today] in the flesh."

Clear as mud? Perhaps not. But we cannot dismiss John's complexity simply because it challenges us. John is so high on this idea that he will repeat it again in his second letter, a book that is so short and rarely quoted that few people can find it without looking at the table of contents first: "Many deceivers have gone out into the world, those who do not confess [the having come and the still coming] of Jesus Christ in the flesh. Such a one is the deceiver and the antichrist" (2 John 7).

such a deceiver is the antichrist

The warnings surrounding this declaration are all the more impactful:

> Watch yourselves, so that you may not lose what we have worked for, but may win a full reward. Everyone who goes on ahead and does not abide in the teaching of Christ, does not have God. Whoever abides in the teaching has both the Father and the Son. (2 John 8–9)

"Abide in Me, and I in you. . . . I am the vine; you are the branches" (John 15:4–5). What does this mean? How do we abide in the διδαχή that Jesus Christ is still coming in the flesh? Where could such a coming happen?

It is possible that John is talking about the "second coming" of Jesus, that great day on which the heavens will be rolled up like a scroll as the archangel shouts and Christians are raised from their graves. But even here it's hard not to hear the echo of Jesus' words from John 6: "Whoever feeds on My flesh and drinks My blood has eternal life, and I will raise him up on the last day" (John 6:54).

There is no escaping the intertwined connection. For Jesus to be in us, for us to be part of His body, for His resurrection to be ours on the Last Day, the actual flesh and blood of Jesus as the new mankind must *come* to us. To deny this is to deny Him. "By this we know that we love the children of God, when we love God and obey His commandments. For this is the love of God, that we keep His commandments. And His commandments are not burdensome" (1 John 5:2–3). It is to reject the new command He gave us when He instituted a New Testament in fulfillment of all ancient prophecy. This is the victory that overcomes the world, that when Jesus speaks unbelievable words about joining Himself to us, about continuing to come to us, we believe them to be true. "This is He who came by water and blood—Jesus Christ; not by the water only but by the water and the blood. And the Spirit is the one who testifies, because the Spirit is the truth" (1 John 5:6).

This is not to say that all people who refuse to believe that Jesus Christ continues to come to us today by means of bread and wine are therefore "the antichrist." But it is to say that they have believed that false spirit's lie. They have chosen burdensome commandments over the new institution of grace alone for faith alone. They are trapped in merely human thinking and in this way are missing out on the most marvelous, tangible promise of Scripture: that when you receive the Lord's Supper, Christ, by the creative power of His promise, is physically choosing to abide in you.

The Spirit Agrees

Hold fast what you have, so that no one
may seize your crown. (Revelation 3:11)

ST. JOHN is concerned with proclaiming the God who is the Word, the God whose Word can be trusted above all other experiences. "If we receive the testimony of men, the testimony of God is greater" (1 John 5:9). But this testimony is more than an abstract idea. This testimony is a Word with flesh, a flesh so purged of man's fallen condition that death no longer has any hold on Him. Through faith alone we believe that this is the Good News of our salvation. But that Good News is no esoteric, flowery talk. "Whoever believes in the Son of God has the testimony in himself" (1 John 5:10). There is a fellowship at work, a common union with the life that is only in the physical flesh and blood of the Son of God. "Whoever does not have the Son of God, does not have life" (1 John 5:12).

Why it has become in vogue for the last five centuries to not believe the testimony that Christ bore concerning Himself on the night before His atoning death is anyone's guess. Yet it's without question that the straightforward meaning of "is" was only the first domino in a long host of doubts that later, well-meaning Christians would raise about the Scriptures. Everyone has a line they draw somewhere, whether it is six-day creation or the definition of marriage or the value of charitable giving and social justice for all people.

"By this we shall know that we are of the truth and reassure our heart" (1 John 3:19). "By this we know that He abides in us" (1 John 3:24). "By this we know the Spirit of truth and the spirit of error" (1 John 4:6; cf. 3:24; 4:13). "By this we know we abide in Him" (1 John 4:13). "By this we know that we love the children of God" (1 John 5:2). "By this we know we have come to know Him, if we keep His commandments" (1 John 2:3; cf. 5:2): when we do not make Him a liar but receive His testimony as greater than our hearts, greater than our minds, as the very words of the God, who knows everything.

death has no hold on this flesh

If our hearts do not condemn us, then we have confidence. We know that in keeping His institutions we are made pleasing to Him. We know that believing in the name of the Son of God and refusing to rebuke Him for His words is to abide in God and have God abide in us.

Literally.

Spiritually.

Physically.

Sacramentally.

Yes.

Jesus once told that woman by the well that "the hour is coming, and is now here, when the true worshipers will worship the Father in spirit and truth" (John 4:23). This

God abides in us, spiritually, physically, sacramentally

does not mean that we are to worship Jesus without His body. This does not mean that we are to worship God without God being located among us. This does not mean abandoning all the fullness of the Son of God's incarnation and continued coming in the flesh.

It does mean exchanging the food that perishes, the mere reasons and possibilities of man's understanding, for the food that endures to eternal life, which is letting God's Word always mean what it says, even when it is marvelous.

"My flesh is true food, and My blood is true drink" (John 6:55).

"How can this man give us His flesh to eat?" (John 6:52). That was the question of unbelief among those to whom Jesus spoke that same day. It was the question of those who later turned back and no longer followed Him, because the saying was too hard for them to allow. That was the question of those who did not abide in His Word, who were no longer His disciples, who therefore did not know the truth, did not have the Spirit giving them life, and as a result were not set free.

I do not believe this means that all Christians in the various rifted Protestant churches that have come to be since the Reformation are therefore not Christians, not believers, and not saved. But I do believe this explains their constant state of decay and endless search for renewal. Having a Word without flesh, they are Christians in churches who, by definition, do not believe that Jesus is among them.

In my own Lutheran tradition, the rise and fall of our outward strength can always be traced to the rise and fall of our sacramental piety. While churches with the name "Lutheran" on the front almost always have books and resources on their shelves that teach the διδαχή of the Lord's Supper, the people and the worship have not always been built on that κοινωνία. With the teaching lost in the dusty corners, other hopes, other silver bullets, other sources of renewal are sought. The more this happens, the greater the peril, the less committed the next generation, and the closer the congregation or body comes to outward collapse.

A lively Christian faith can endure a lifetime without the proper teaching of the Lord's Supper. But a lively Christian **Church** cannot. To be sure, an active organization, busy assembling a missionary fervor for conversions or mercy, can be stirred up among even the most crass pagans and atheists. If these are our outward signs of life, we might never know that something is amiss. But a Church that continues to produce new generations of Christians who find their life source in the blood of Jesus of Nazareth, who could not imagine any other faith, any other religion, any other mystery—this only comes from dynamic attention to the details of Jesus' words: "Sanctify them in the truth; Your word is truth" (John 17:17).

Church cannot endure without the proper teaching of the Lord's Supper

"Whoever says 'I know Him' but does not keep His commandments is a liar, and the truth is not in him, but whoever keeps His word, in him truly the love of God is perfected" (1 John 2:4–5). "This is He who came by water and blood—Jesus Christ; not by the water only but by the water and the blood. And the Spirit is the one who testifies, because the Spirit is the truth" (1 John 5:6). "Whoever does not believe God has made Him a liar, because he has not believed in the testimony that God has borne concerning His Son" (1 John 5:10). "Everyone who goes on ahead and does not abide in the teaching of Christ, does not have God" (2 John 9). 🐟

What (on Earth!) Is Jesus Doing?

The only thing that might be construed as missing from the Words of Institution would be an explanation of *how it is possible* for the bread he held in his hands to be his body. . . . Yet Jesus did not offer such an explanation on the occasion of any of his miracles.

Hermann Sasse

Manifoldly does Christ initiate us by these words. . . . His Discourse is hard of attainment by the more unlearned, asking for itself rather the understanding of faith than investigation.

Cyril of Alexandria

Do you know when the mountain goats give birth? . . . Is it by your understanding that the hawk soars . . . ? Shall a faultfinder contend with the Almighty? . . . Will you condemn Me that you may be in the right?

Jesus of Nazareth, Son of God

Mission, Stated

> Why is it thought incredible by any of
> you that God raises the dead? (Acts 26:8)

I STILL remember vividly a group project that I had to complete at the seminary. We were tasked with coming up with a statement to summarize the life of a congregation. Mission statements had been all the rage in American business about thirty years before, and in good form, the LCMS had decided it was the newest, most necessary thing. Eager to prove my mettle and demonstrate that we could craft a classic mission statement for a congregation that nonetheless had some real biblical meat to it, I convinced my three group-work classmates to embrace and submit the following:

[Awesomesauce] Lutheran Church: Raising the dead
with the Word and Sacraments of Jesus Christ.

We received a C+.

I was dumbfounded.

I still am.

The criticism, when I confronted my professor, was that the statement was not *specific* enough. I believe I know what he meant. By specific, he meant something the people in the pew could look at themselves doing. He wanted something we could test. Certainly, Christians in a Lutheran congregation do not *see* themselves rising from the dead at any point, especially after they partake of the Lord's Supper.

Point taken. But it's the *wrong* point.

There is nothing more specific, nothing more particular, nothing more scandalously evident, than the eating of bread and wine in a communal meal. This goes double when one practices the biblical mandate of closed Communion. When that happens, the event is so specific, so unifying, so evidently effective, that it creates immediate and outright offense to those who are asked to stay away!

It is hard to be more specific about the purpose of our congregations than to believe it's to eat and drink the bread and wine that grant us the gift of immortality. But this also illustrates the very point of our near collapse as Protestants. We long for the Spirit and presence of Jesus. We write new songs, amplify our efforts at charity and outreach, scour the Scriptures for a trick or insight or point to make everything click better—and we do it all because we do not deeply believe the scandalously specific nature of Jesus' final words of the Great Commission: As you go, make disciples, baptizing and teaching; "And behold, I am with you always, to the end of the age" (Matthew 28:20).

This isn't fuzzy talk. This is present, direct, meaning-filled promise.

There is another vivid memory I have of a joke that I was given by an agnostic friend in college. She was a kindhearted poet, a self-proclaimed bisexual who would have been at home on a Harley-Davidson with her husband riding behind her. Despite our philosophical differences, we were good friends and respected each other. So at graduation, she presented me with a greeting card. At the time, I was too prudish to see the humor in it, though now I find that it's pretty funny after all. It was a garish orange, with the silhouette of a yellow couch drawn on the front. Behind the couch, there was a second silhouette, a long-haired man in robe-like clothing with his arms raised to the sky. The words beneath him read, "I found Jesus! He was under the couch the entire time!"

raising the dead with the Sacraments of Jesus

It was later at the seminary that the deep insight of the joke struck me, when I heard a tale about a famously obtuse professor. He was the kind of guy whom the students either loved or hated. Because he retired from full-time teaching before I completed my studies, I was never able to sit at his feet. But as the story goes, one day all of the students for a particular class came into his classroom only to find him, bespectacled and dressed in his normal dapper attire, down on his hands and knees in the corner of the room as if searching for a dropped pen or paper clip.

Student after student entered the room, each seeing him there, and one after another assuming he'd only just gotten down on the ground the moment before they entered. But eventually the whole room was full and the bell to begin studies rang. But the professor stayed down on the ground in the corner, avidly moving his head and hands about, sweeping the ground and searching for something he clearly could not find. At last, so the story goes, perhaps some five or ten minutes after class should have begun, well after everyone else had made eye contact more than a few times and shared a great deal of shrugging and confused sign language, someone got bold enough to pipe up and ask if the poor old dodder needed any help.

"Without the Lord's Supper," the wizened and skinny man suddenly shouted, his face still inches from the tile and moving about, "where *does* one find Jesus?"

without the Lord's Supper, where does one find Jesus?

You Cannot Serve Two Masters

> Charge them before God not to quarrel about words, which does no good, but only ruins the hearers.
> (2 Timothy 2:14)

ONE OF THE most common arguments against the sacramental presence of Jesus in the Supper is the objection that His body was already present at the table as He spoke the words. "Since Jesus was clearly sitting there, holding the bread in His hand," so the argument goes, "it is evident that His whole body was attached to His hand. Therefore, it could not possibly have been in the bread."

This is all very logical. It is all very well-meant. It does not intend to undo the existence of the Church. Yet it also does not bother to use Scripture as its foundation. Confronted by the Word of God, the argument's disbelief jumps straight to human thinking without even bothering to flinch.

There is nothing in the Bible that teaches that limitations are built into the human body that prevent it from being present in more than one place at once. There are no passages dictating that the incarnate God is limited in His powers regarding the material creation. Nothing in the Bible says, "Jesus cannot do more with a human body than the average man can." In fact, the whole New Testament is a valiant thesis to the contrary!

The point here, however, is not the argument itself. The point is the almost unseen, perhaps inadvertent shift *away* from the text of Scripture. "But Jesus was sitting there" is not a reference to a Bible verse that teaches His words cannot mean what they say. It is a reference to logical philosophy.

There is nothing wrong with logical philosophy. But there is something wrong with using it as if it were a biblical argument. There is something drastically wrong with not admitting that our position on the meaning of a given Scripture is not founded on Scripture but on a supreme trust in our understanding. There is something substantially wrong with placing limitations on Jesus' body because we believe that human reason is ultimately unlimited in its capacity to understand all things.

With a swift flourish, like a magician distracting you with hand motions as he slides a card from his sleeve, the argument is too tickled with its own cleverness to even realize that it is also a full denial of the principle of Scripture alone. This is why, after five hundred years of division and decay in the churches, we who stand at this precipice must slow down. We must take notice not only of the arguments but, more important, of *the approach* that has driven us into them. To fail to do this is to forever submit ourselves to unintentional delusion at the whims of the "plausible arguments" (Colossians 2:4) Paul warns us against. It is to fail to "take every thought captive to obey Christ," and to allow "arguments and every lofty opinion raised against the knowledge of God" (2 Corinthians 10:5), all because we are too hasty to set our minds against the revelations of the mind of Christ.

whimsical delusions flourish behind plausible arguments

There is a proverb I have heard, though I cannot find any record of it on Google, so perhaps it's not a true proverb. It goes, "If the master urinates while walking, the disciple will urinate while running." Perhaps the sourcing has been limited by the potty humor of the matter, but the point is so profound that we should not miss it! What you or I might do easily and without making any evident mess, another who has less self-control and a greater zeal to prove himself might do to the extreme, resulting in unequivocal catastrophe.

You may indeed be able to doubt a biblical verse or three without harming your faith in the resurrection and justification of Jesus. You may be firmly convinced that having these doubts is merely reasonable. But what you will pass on to those who listen to you will not be the individual reasons you believe all the other verses in the Scriptures. What you will teach by your choice is the first principle that all men are free to decide for themselves which verses to keep and which verses to toss out. Within a generation or so, the most obvious truths, the ones that you never dreamed of questioning, will likewise find themselves under suspicion. By the power of your principle of reason, all that the Bible holds will eventually be relegated to mythology, bigotry, or old-fashioned ignorance.

he does not invite the pigs into the house

The good news in all this mess is that the eternal message of Jesus is always more powerful than us, even than our doubts. The words of God are always more powerful than the most self-destructive blindness we can drum up. "If we are faithless, He remains faithful—for He cannot deny Himself" (2 Timothy 2:13).

If we should find ourselves sleeping among the pigs in a foreign land, the Father of our house treats even His servants with great mercy. There is always the open possibility of return. Returning, we always find the Father overjoyed, putting a ring on our finger, new shoes on our feet, and slaughtering the fatted calf in celebration.

At the same time, a return to our Father's house always means a return to His actual words. When the father in the parable shouts, "This my son was dead, and is alive again; he was lost, and is found" (Luke 15:24), he is not inviting the pigs into the house. We are called to leave the doubt, avoid the deception, reject the misdirection, and condemn unbelief to remain outside the gates.

When we attend to the Scriptures alone as our foundation, we find that there is no verse in the Bible that teaches us to believe that a man cannot be in two places at once. Much less does any verse in the Bible teach us that God cannot do with His creation whatever He wants to do with it. This goes not less but *more* for His own body.

Jesus walked on water. Jesus disappeared from crowded spaces and appeared in locked rooms. Jesus talked to fevers and they listened to Him.

He touched lepers and they did not give Him leprosy. He made water become wine without grapes anywhere nearby.

Jesus read minds. Jesus glowed. Jesus ascended out of space and into the highest immanent heaven of the trinitarian union.

will we be studiously Christian?

With which of these many texts of Scripture do we arm ourselves as we ask the question of whether or not He is able give of Himself with His own hand?

History is clear that skeptical men will always keep asking. Like the cranky brother in the parable, they will stand outside the feast and ramble on about the feast they would have preferred to have. This will not stop them from being the Father's sons, at least not directly. But it will prevent them from knowing the magnificent κοινωνία of the Father's house. It will condemn the Ἐγώ εἰμι of "I am with you always" to mere metaphor. It will prevent them from ever experiencing grace as anything more than a *symbol*.

If we will be studiously Christian, if we will pass our Christianity on to our children after us, then what we believe about Christianity must be founded on the *text* of the Bible rather than on our interpretations of it. The poorly adopted habit of bickering over the meanings of words will not do. We are talking about "the words of eternal life" (John 6:68). They have not been given to us in order to sow discord. They are given to be believed.

If we lift up human reason as the final beacon that illuminates the Scriptures, it will not be faith but doubt that we create. The fires of dissension burn on the fuel of human speculations, stripping the Bible of its meat, leaving behind a charred body of meaningless signs. We should not be surprised that churches do not long sustain themselves on such a humanly devised significance. We should not be shocked that churches cannot live on a Word without flesh.

The Church Is Not a Question

But the fruit of the Spirit is . . . patience. (Galatians 5:22)

The fruit of the Spirit is not passion but love. Not success but joy. Not chaos but peace. The fruit of the Spirit is not victory but self-control. Not action but gentleness. Not change but faithfulness.

The Spirit of Jesus does not save us from despair only to deliver us into hysteria. Nor are we given to be driven about by every storm and wind of teaching about the many threats to us. Our devotion is grounded on firmer stuff than that. What may appear crucial to our minds, what may seem a threat, should the earth open itself to swallow us whole and the heavens fall like fury into the seas, the Holy Spirit of Jesus grants us not the fruit of change but the fruit of *patience*. Such true spirituality grants the Church of Jesus something even more audacious, even more radical, even more resolute. The real fruit of the Spirit is not *change* but the ability to *wait*.

The authentic Church of Jesus can wait patiently because we know that for us there is no such thing as a true crisis. There is work to be done. There are actions to take. There are dangers to avoid. But there is never a change we have to make. Nothing exists that should ever cause us to fear for our future, because we know that the Church of Jesus Christ *is* Jesus.

And Jesus is *alive*.

And Jesus is *in charge*.

We do not lead. We *follow*.

We do not save. We are *given* salvation.

We do not change. We *remember*.

We do not go out on a mission of saving others. We are charged to tell others of every race and language that thanks to the work of Jesus, they are already *saved*.

the Church of Jesus Christ *is* Jesus

Christianity is the religion of *believing* this. At its root, Christian faith is an undying conviction that death cannot touch us. The sting has been clipped. An empty form alone remains. When they strike us down, we only become stronger. When one Christian is cut down, two more rise to take his place. The history of mission is always watered by the blood of the martyrs. Yet the more we die, the more we come alive to live. Rains can fall and floods can come, but the house will not fall because it is built on a rock. That rock always has been and is *still* Christ.

There is nothing we need to do to make this certain. It is a matter of faith alone. These are promises given in order that they may be believed. Not us alone but these words will weather every storm, quench every fire, and cease the quaking of every heart. When these words are among us, so is He, even to the end of the ages.

In any and every circumstance, the fruit of the Spirit that is patience benefits us with a calm willingness to face down the end of lives, the end of a congregation, or the end of all things with a powerful and meaningful resolve to gladly do **nothing** about it, to "Be still, and know that" Jesus "will be exalted among the nations" (Psalm 46:10). Nothing in heaven or earth can stop this.

When such words are removed from our center, when we receive them with a pious but self-righteous "yes, but," then such doubt places us into an entirely different story. Without Jesus among us as the guarantee that we cannot die, all manner of temporal worry quickly descends. Without Jesus, or with Jesus far away off in heaven, the certain "This is" of every word from Him is replaced with the gaping vacuum of "maybe," "if only," and "as if."

This is why ἑτερο-διδαχή is always in such a rush. In part, it's a learned tactic, a trick for avoiding suspicion. When one is howling at the moon about the falling sky, people take less time to test your claims in the panic that ensues. But it is not as though these howlers do not believe their own mythologies. They are not crass liars but deceived believers. They, too, then, are driven more than most by a manic need, a frenzy rooted in authentic, fear-filled self-reliance. The more they see their own shoulders as the foundation for the churches, the more they see the looming possibility of collapse. The more the potential for failure arises, the more hasty their quest and feverish their howling becomes.

It is a sandy land that exists once the rock has been removed. When we find ourselves in such a state, the antidote is not to change more but to change less. Or to put it more accurately, to change **back**. For us today, this must begin by putting the Lord's Supper back into its proper place as God's antidote to our impatience and fear. This is the activity that Jesus has inspired with His almighty authority. This is where His hands are firmly on the wheel and shall never be shaken.

Faith Is Power

> He breaks the bow and shatters the spear. . . .
> "Be still and know that [He is] God." (Psalm 46:9–10)

REAL CHURCH is what happens when we believe that we are not alone because Jesus has insisted that He will not let us be alone. Real Church is what happens because Jesus has, without us, refused to keep the resurrection of His body all to Himself. Real Church is what happens where Jesus sets Himself down in our midst, beyond all that we could ask or imagine, for the sole purpose of compelling us to believe that in Him the impossible (our salvation) has become the God-spoken truth.

This is a radical reversal. Not only are sin, death, and the devil's power flipped on their heads, but so, too, are all our works, thoughts, and ways. Now, a mere two or three of us, armed with God's Word alone, are more than conquerors because the One who loves us is there in our midst, strong to save. With such promises to rest upon, the threat of unbeatable storms shall only entrench us further in our convictions. With such certainty to build our house upon, the perils of violent death shall not deter us. No matter how high the waves become, they are only a reminder of the vast power of our little boat to never leak, never capsize, and never run ashore, because our pilot is Jesus. Even if it appears to us that He is sleeping in the stern, our senses deceive us. He has the words to prove that all things are well in His hand.

Those things that might cause us despair? In Jesus' body, they are refiner's fire to bolster our strength. Those things that may terrorize us? In Jesus' blood, they are fuller's soap to purify our courage. Those things that would distract us from the certainty of our God's words? In the bread and wine on the altar, they are opportunities to confess our resolve.

We may indeed face physical torment. We may indeed endure great losses, even of human life. We may well be sent to our death, for this has happened before in many times and various places. But "precious in the sight of the LORD is the death of His saints" (Psalm 116:15).

Jesus in our midst is both impossible and true

None of these things put us under pressure to react in haste. None of these things are reasons to abandon our glorious and successful past of standing firm. None of these things are ultimately our concern. Of course, we must handle the day's business. Of course, we must pay the bills. "If you can gain your freedom, avail yourself of the opportunity" (1 Corinthians 7:21). But know that rise or fall, live or die, grow or shrink, none of it is "worth comparing with the glory that is to be revealed to us" (Romans 8:18).

We have a future that is unavoidable. **We. Cannot. Die.** The Church of Jesus' Christianity is the physical manifestation of this promise in the world. We are, by faith in the specific words of the Supper itself, the resurrected body of Jesus. What is there that could trouble us? What is there that could make us be afraid?

real Church cannot die

Bad Mission

> In the presence of God and of Christ Jesus and of the elect angels I charge you to keep these rules without prejudging. (1 Timothy 5:21)

JESUS MET with His disciples on a mountaintop in Galilee. What He had in mind was beyond their imagination. Yet before He ascended, leaving them behind to die martyrs' deaths, He commissioned them to a specific task. He gave them clear and demonstrative words to initiate a summary rule of faith and life while they sojourned on this earth. He said:

All authority in heaven and on earth has been given to Me. Go therefore and make disciples of all nations, baptizing them in the name of the Father and of the Son and of the Holy Spirit, teaching them to observe all that I have commanded you. (Matthew 28:18–20)

All authority. Jesus promised us that there is nothing that He cannot do. There is no reality so reasonable that He cannot alter it. He both created the universe and redeemed the universe. By both actions He demonstrates His almighty power to manipulate the fabric of reality according to His designs. With such real, ultimate power at His command, what did He intend to do with it? What does He intend for His Church to do?

Disciple. The "go" in this Matthew 28 is another of those "-ing" participles. It is an action word that isn't so much a command as a description.

It is perfectly fine to translate the text "go and disciple," but the emphasis is not on the going. It is on the discipling. It is like He said, "While you go, where you go, as you go, whenever you go, **disciple**."

This is more than "making disciples" and deeper even than a conversion moment. It's the Lord's *discipline*. It's the life of Christian immortalizing. But how? Where? What does it look like? For that, two more "-ing" participles are attached in order to add flesh to the institution.

Baptizing. This has not been a book about Baptism, nor will it start to be now. Baptism is its own massive topic, severely misunderstood and underutilized in our present age. But for our purpose, it's enough to notice that making disciples happens with *two* different types of discipline. Jesus announced that all authority to discipline the nations came down to two tools that He left us for the making of all Christian faith. These tools are *never* without each other. They are complementary. As John has already told us, the Spirit and the water agree.

Teaching . . . observe all that I have commanded. This is the meat and drink indeed! It is the διδαχή, along with the water, which does these things, for the sake of the faithful who will believe them. Getting people wet with water without teaching any words is a fool's errand. It is like gathering the largest assembly you've ever seen, calling it Church, and never bothering to open the Bible. It is like giving birth to a baby but never bothering to feed him.

This means that Christians are not free to be Christians without the Scriptures. The Scriptures are the power to make and hold us as Christians. It has always been this way. The history of failed churches is the history of those who have lost first a jot, then an iota, then a word, then a paragraph and more until, even though the words have not passed away, those churches' faith has.

Rare indeed is the congregation or assembly that is not fearfully worried about getting more people saved. I have yet to meet the people who are not concerned about their neighbors, their friends, and their children. But I have been to many, many congregations that cannot tell me much about the life we want to save people *into*.

In the many books on missiology and church leadership that I have been exposed to over the years, both as a seminarian and a pastor, I have come across mission books that put their emphasis on everything from constitutions to guitars, from communism to rolling on the ground like a dog. But I have never come across one that says, "We need to get the Lord's Supper right."

This is to our peril. Whether it has happened because we have become hungry for glory, or distracted by propaganda, or so desperate that any idol will do, we all find ourselves in the same boat. As a whole, as Protestantism, we have lost sight of a key insight given by St. Paul: a thousand people hearing five thousand words of Scripture that they do not understand is far less powerful than a mere two or three gathered in the name of Jesus and believing the whole lot of it. When a congregation authentically trusts that the Holy Meal of Jesus is our unity with each other in God, we become new creations, so marvelously ecstatic that the individual members can't help but talk about being the Body of Christ.

from communism to rolling on the ground like a dog

"Take and eat. This is My body." It's just a few more than five words. But it is also the true and lasting mission of the Church. While our ragged and decaying reformation lurches onward, flirting with revivalism, reviving with moralism, moralizing with liberalism, and then liberally embracing paganism, the διδαχή is a beacon to which we must rally. No matter how grave the situation may feel or seem, returning in heartfelt contrition to the observance of everything Jesus commanded is a unifying vision of redemption. "Do this" (Luke 22:19).

Only the Unbelievable Will Do

He who has ears to hear, let him hear.
(Matthew 11:15)

A SUPERNATURAL thing, by definition, can only be *believed*. To believe in miracles is to believe in things beyond the mind. It is not only that we have not discovered an explanation. It is that *there is no explanation*.

This is nothing new. The God who is, the God who created the world out of nothing in just a few days, has never been in the business of explaining Himself to us. He has never been in the business of giving us words to test.

But He has **always** been in the business of giving us promises to be believed.

This was the value of the trees in the midst of the garden that Adam and his wife were forbidden to touch. This was not a trick to see if His perfect creation might be capable of falling, nor some obtuse proof for discovering whether or not Adam would willingly love Him. This was the gift of words that could **only** be believed.

When God said, "In the day that you eat of it you shall surely die" (Genesis 2:17), He was ensuring Adam that he could **not** die. He was promising that mankind was owed every experience in the universe with the exception of the knowledge of evil. Until the temptation, by faith we believed this.

But when Adam reached out his hand and took the fruit of not waiting, the fruit of impatience, the fruit of needing to understand, he did so by rejecting faith in the plain meaning of the words of his God. He tried to see them. He attempted to test them. He thought he could disprove them. With a hurried and bold act of change, all was undone.

Christianity is the religion given by God to restore what was lost: faith in the words that cannot be proven. Faith alone is what died in Adam. Faith alone is what Christ's promise restores. Trust in the plain meaning of God's unbelievable words **is** eternal life.

You cannot "believe alone" in what you understand. You can hope for what you see. You cannot overcome faithlessness with reason. All attempts to see into the hidden majesty of the mind of God can only further wreck what little capacity we've retained. But God, without us, by supernatural declarations, has promised us the answer we would never have looked for, because the unimaginable is exactly what the regeneration of faith needs.

trust in God's word is eternal life

Nowhere is this more evident than in the eating and drinking of bread and wine in His Most Holy Meal. There, God grants to us a word that we know, by definition, cannot possibly be true. Jesus makes a claim that is infinitely beyond us. He declares a truth that is factually unbelievable. But it's precisely that unbelievability, guaranteed by a trustworthy source, that we so desperately need. It is precisely a supernatural truth that is required to arouse in us the audacity of faith alone. ❧

The Solution of Not Doing

Patience is one of the things that distinguishes the Church from the sect. The sect must have everything at once. It cannot wait, because it has no future. The Church can wait, because it has a future.

Hermann Sasse

You are fond of contention, brothers, and full of zeal about things which do not pertain to salvation. Look carefully to the Scriptures, which are the true utterances of the Holy Spirit.

Clement, Bishop of Rome

I am with you always.

Jesus of Nazareth, son of Mary

God Died

Eat the flesh ... drink His blood. (John 6:53)

"*THIS IS*" is a religion. But it is no religious precept.

"This is" is a cry of command. But it is no commandment.

You cannot obey "This is." You cannot allegorize it. "This is" teaches no morality.

"This is" cannot be applied. "This is" cannot even be truly considered.

"This is" is an ***event***. A day. A moment. An apex, under which history itself was crushed, and all of us along with it.

God: crucified.

The Almighty: powerless.

The unlimited: circumscribed.

Justice: condemned.

The infinite: finitized.

Life: dead.

"This shall never happen" (Matthew 16:22).

But it did.

"This is" is altogether ***alien***. Foreign. So insane that the only reasonable argument that has ever been brought against it is that "it can't be true because it can't be true."

"It's impossible."

That's the best we can do.

Rank unbelief.

A myriad of historic witnesses present an all but undeniable case, and "I refuse to believe that it makes sense" is the best closing argument the scholars and debaters of the age can come up with.

I agree with them. "This is" is madness. It surpasses all thought and fantasy. But for me, "This is" is an argument in its favor.

Who is the greater fool? The one who believes in a God who achieves the unfathomable, or the one who only believes in a god whom he can wrap his mind around? In the end, the most reasonable religion is the one with a God whose purposes surpass our own, whose nature defies our logic, whose ways are higher than our ways, and whose thoughts are higher than our thoughts.

Only a massive arrogance could claim that a God with the capabilities to create a universe such as ours would then be limited to the rules of that universe. In this way, a religion becomes most suspect if it never makes any claim upon us that appears from our vantage point to be lunacy or, to use a more classic term, supernatural. Such a neutered spirituality is a counterfeit religion that only teaches what natural minds can conceive, dream up, and accomplish on our own.

When Jesus took death into Himself by being taken into it, He did not make God more understandable than He was before. He eternally demanded of us the belief that the nature of God is beyond our understanding. We shall never fathom Him. We shall never be His teacher. He is the author of the rules for the game and for every other new game He shall ever start. When He speaks, all bets are off. What we think, what we are willing to conceive, is no longer the referee. It is the *opponent*.

Christianity, before it is anything else, is a condemnation of our ability to be our own judges. From its most fundamental premise, Christianity is a religion that is beyond the scope of our minds. The "This is" of the Christ who "**must suffer**" and be "the first to rise from the dead" (Acts 26:23, emphasis added) is not something we are capable of making up. It is too preposterous for even the most wild-eyed oracle. It is too falsifiable for the most reckless charlatan. It is too absurd for the daftest mythology. It is either self-admittedly desperate insanity or the verbal revelation of a radically holy God.

Believing this, what greater madness still is it to question any other revelation from His mouth? Jesus of Nazareth is the God who both died and rose from the dead. It is high time that the modern Christian Church work a little harder to own the *mystery* of it. It is time to believe that the impossible claims of Christianity are not accidental but fundamental. It is time to consider that our modern attempts to domesticate the words that Jesus has left us have amounted to a denial of them.

He did not make God more under-standable

"this is" the verbal revelation of a radically holy God

Because we are the Church, even these gray and latter-day trials are not a true threat to us. Because we are the Body of Christ, we shall revive. Because the testimony of the water and the blood are in agreement with the words of the eternal Spirit, Jesus is not far off but very near. The bread and wine are on the table. The Words of Institution are the physical presence of Jesus. He does not sow division but unity. He does not plant confusion but peace.

It is high time that we stop trying to grasp the sacramental words of Jesus with our minds and exhibit the spiritual patience to wait upon them.

To wait and to repeat.

To keep saying.

Keep listening.

Keep remembering.

"This is" is no guess.

"This is" is no gimmick.

"This is" is no gamble.

Our Lord has always had a plan.

An extremely specific vision.

A marvelously peculiar mission.

A single, scandalously particular, highly unbelievable, certified, eternal *promise*.

"Do *this*."

"This is" is κοινωνία. Kneel down, put out your hand, and say, "Amen." ✦

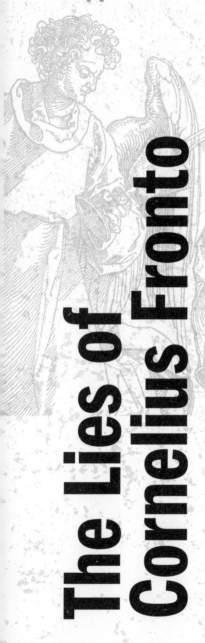

The Lies of Cornelius Fronto

Assemble yourselves together in common, every one of you . . . man by man, in grace, in one faith and one Jesus Christ, who after the flesh was of David's race, who is Son of Man and Son of God, to the end that ye may obey the bishop and presbytery without distraction of mind; breaking one bread, which is the medicine of immortality and the antidote that we should not die but live forever in Jesus Christ.

Ignatius of Antioch

Seeing, touching, tasting are in thee deceived How says trusty hearing? That shall be believed What God's Son has told me, take for truth I do; Truth himself speaks truly or there's nothing true.

Thomas Aquinas

No sign testifies with such infallible certainty the death throes of a congregation, or a whole church, as the decline and decay of the celebration of the Eucharist. This is, however, the deadly serious situation in which a very large segment of these Protestant churches of the world finds itself.

What constitutes the essence of [church] community is not what it has in common with other communities, but what distinguishes it from them.

Hermann Sasse

The Lies of Cornelius Fronto

MARCUS CORNELIUS FRONTO was a Roman citizen who was a famed lawyer and orator, second only, it was said, to the well-known Cicero. He not only served in the political office of Consul, but he was appointed by the Emperor Antoninus Pius to tutor his young and later famous son Marcus Aurelius.

He was no friend of Christianity, and he did his best to spread abroad the horrors of early Christian worship by writing,

- A young baby is covered with flour, the object being to deceive the unwary. It is then served to the person to be admitted into the rites. The recruit is urged to inflict blows onto it. . . . The baby is killed with wounds that remain unseen and concealed.

- It is the blood of this infant—I shudder to mention it—it is this blood that they lick with thirsty lips; these are the limbs they distribute eagerly; this is the victim by which they seal their covenant. . . .

- On a special day they gather in a feast with all . . . sexes and ages. There, flushed with the banquet after such feasting and drinking, they begin to burn with incestuous passions. They provoke a dog tied to the lamp . . . [until] the light is overturned and extinguished, and, with it, common knowledge of their actions, in the shameless dark, with unspeakable lust, they copulate in random unions, all equally being guilty of incest, some by deed, but everyone by complicity.

From this slander it's evident that the early Christian age confronted a world no more willing to understand our position than they are today. The worst kind of lies and atrocities were readily believed as excuses for avoiding honest confrontation with the revealed Word. But as is the case in more than one circumstance, this "hostile witness" has provided us with a very keen insight into the ongoing misunderstanding of early Christianity. Somewhere, someone got the crazy idea that when they got together on Sundays, they would do so in order to drink "the blood of a son of man."

Justin Martyr's Response

JUSTIN MARTYR is one of the first Church Fathers, and his writings are some of the earliest that we have available after the New Testament Scriptures themselves. Born around AD 100 in Samaria, he lived a thoroughly pagan life until his conversion to Christianity, having become convinced of its superiority in both morality and spirituality. During the reign of Antoninus Pius, he started a school for philosophy in Rome, and so he was well positioned to confront the lies of Cornelius Fronto head on.

This he did in his *First Apology*, his *Second Apology*, his *Dialogue with Trypho* and a number of other works. During the reign of Marcus Aurelius, his teaching and faith offended the well-known cynic philosopher Crescens, who denounced him to the authorities. He was summarily tried, convicted, and beheaded, but not before leaving us the following:

- This food is called among us the Eucharist, of which no one is allowed to partake except one who believes that the things we teach are true, and has received the washing that is for the remission of sins and for rebirth, and show a life as Christ handed down. . . .

- For we do not receive these things as common bread nor common drink, but, in like manner as Jesus Christ our Savior—having been incarnate by God's Word, took both flesh and blood for our salvation—from him, from which our blood and flesh are nourished by transformation, is the flesh and blood of that Jesus who became incarnate. . . .

- For the Apostles in the memoirs composed by them, which are called Gospels, thus handed down what was commanded them: that Jesus took bread, and having given thanks said, "Do this for my memorial. This is my body." And likewise, he took the chalice and, having given thanks, said, "This is my blood." And [he] gave it to them alone. . . .

- The wicked demons have imitated [this] in the mysteries of Mithra, and handed [it] down to be done. For [there] bread and . . . water are placed with certain words said over them in the secret rites of initiation. . . . [But] this elevated and pure tone was not maintained. . . . Naturalistic, mystical elements usurped this communion with Jesus . . . [and] crept in, from the undercurrent of popular religion. . . . The first beginnings of this fateful development manifest themselves already in Paul.[4]

---

4   The First Apology of Justin Martyr, 66.

THE WORDS of the Fathers are not in themselves an argument. Scripture alone is our sufficiency. But it's marvelous to see that the crimson thread of the sacramental mystery is no invention of the Dark Ages foisted upon the churches thanks to superstition. In the very earliest years after the apostles, one of the most visible defenders of the faith, who himself would shed his blood rather than recant it, confessed before the world the same words that were handed to Paul.

This bread. This wine. Uncommon. Holy. No beauty we could desire. Our God. ❧

Sources of Chapter Headings and Poetry

OPENING PAGES

ALL ATTEMPTS to build Christian congregations without placing at their center the congregation-forming Sacrament of the Altar are just as much condemned to failure as are efforts to renew the Divine Service without renewing the Lord's Supper. The sad experiences of the nineteenth and twentieth centuries in this area only confirm the lessons of the past. The enormous effort made in the area of church planting during recent generations must be regarded as a failure. It has produced a wealth of societies and card files. . . . They have produced liturgies galore for every conceivable taste, but they have hitherto proved unable to move people to go to church again in order to celebrate these liturgies. Where the custom of church-going has lapsed with the consequence that the Christian congregation is dead or dying, there is but one single means for getting people back to church. Hunger and thirst for the Lord's Supper must be aroused in them. Hermann Sasse, "Church and Lord's Supper," *The Lonely Way*, vol. 1, p. 395.

INTRODUCTION: THE CRISIS OF CROSSLESSNESS

1. What is wrong with our church? What is wrong with each one of us and our faith if such disintegration of our church was possible? Dr. Hermann Sasse, *The Lonely Way*, vol. 2, "The Crisis of Lutheranism," p. 270.

2. *Quid incertitudine imserius*? [What is more wretched than uncertainty?] Martin Luther, *On the Bondage of the Will*, p. 15.[5]

3. Jesus Christ is the same yesterday and today and forever. (Hebrews:13:8)

CHAPTER 1: THE PROBLEM OF NOT DOING

1. Evangelical theology's burning wound . . . is that skepticism which no longer believes the Scriptures to be the Word of God. Hermann Sasse, "Church and Lord's Supper," *The Lonely Way*, vol. 1, pp. 321–22.

2. For the sake of my person and life I will humble myself before anyone and beg grace and favor from a child insofar as these people are not hostile to the Gospel. For I know that if it is strictly judged, my life earns nothing but the abyss of hell. But for the sake of my office and doctrine, and even of my life to the extent that it comes to these, let no one—particularly tyrants and persecutors of the Gospel—expect any patience or humility from me. Martin Luther, *Auf des Königs zu England Lästerschrift Titel*, WA 23:26–37, p. 34.

3. All mankind are liars. (Psalm 116:11)

CHAPTER 2: WHERE MIGHT JESUS BE?

1. If we do not take what Scripture says concerning the presence of Christ with complete seriousness, then we have a wrong understanding of Christ. Then we also have a wrong understanding of his church. Then we have a mental construct of Christ in place of the real Christ, and in place of the real church, in which Jesus Christ is really present according to both his divinity *and* his humanity, we have a dream church, a mere community of spirits in which Christ is only spiritually present just as he was prior to his incarnation. Hermann Sasse, "Church and Lord's Supper," *The Lonely Way*, vol. 1, pp. 428–29.

---

5   Sasse, *The Lonely Way*, vol. 1, p. 388, footnote.

2. Where Christ is, there is the Church. Ignatius of Antioch, *Letter to the Smyrneans*, chap. 8.

3. In the place that He will choose, to make His name dwell there, you shall eat the tithe of your grain, of your wine. (Deuteronomy 14:23)

CHAPTER 3: WHERE HAS JESUS BEEN?

1. It is a matter of faith. Hermann Sasse, "Church and Lord's Supper," *The Lonely Way*, vol. 1, p. 424.

2. God does not present us with any incomprehensible propositions. Ulrich Zwingli, AE 38:21.

3. Who has made man's mouth? (Exodus 4:11)

CHAPTER 4: WHAT MORE COULD JESUS DO?

1. The claim that the greatest, most profound, and most all-encompassing community of human history has been established by these unimpressive-looking Sacraments is just as offensive to our thinking as is the assertion that God's Holy Spirit is given along this path. And yet this is the case. For this reason, the church herself remains an insoluble riddle for human reason, a pure article of faith. Hermann Sasse, "Church and Lord's Supper," *The Lonely Way*, vol. 1, p. 406.

2. The question is, "Where is the Church?" What, therefore, are we to do? Are we to seek it in our own words or in the words of its Head, our Lord Jesus Christ? I think that we ought to seek it in the words of Him who is Truth, and who knows His own body best. Augustine of Hippo, *Against the Donatists*, IV, 15:2.

3. Let there be light. (Genesis 1:3)

CHAPTER 5: WHAT MORE COULD JESUS HAVE SAID?

1. Scripture alone bears responsibility for the indisputably paradoxical nature of the assertions made in the eucharistic dogma. . . . A valid reason to depart from the literal understanding [ought] never be found in a philosophical argument against the possibility. . . . The one and only justification for abandoning the literal sense would be the existence of a word of Scripture that teaches a different understanding. Hermann Sasse, "Church and Lord's Supper," *The Lonely Way*, vol. 1, pp. 406–7.

2. Consequently, you can boldly address Christ both in the hour of death and at the Last Judgment: "My dear Lord Jesus Christ, a controversy has arisen over thy words. . . . I have remained with thy text as the words read. If there is anything obscure in them, it is because thou didst wish to leave it obscure, for thou hast given no other explanation." Martin Luther, "Confession Concerning Christ's Supper," AE 37:305.

3. I appeal to you, brothers, by the name of our Lord Jesus Christ, that all of you agree, and that there be no divisions among you, but that you be united in the same mind and the same judgment. (1 Corinthians 1:10)

CHAPTER 6: WHAT DID JESUS ACTUALLY SAY?

1. The cause of strife . . . does not lie in the Lord's Words but in the doubt of people who do not want to believe him in these words. Hermann Sasse, "Church and Lord's Supper," *The Lonely Way*, vol. 1, p. 404.

2. Seeing, touching, tasting—are in thee deceived; How says trusty hearing? That shall be believed! What God's Son has told me, take for truth I do. Truth himself speaks truly, or there is nothing true. Thomas Aquinas, *Catechism of the Catholic Church*, 1381.[6]

3. Be still, and know that I am God. (Psalm 46:10)

CHAPTER 7: WHAT DID PAUL RECEIVE?

1. It is not a superfluous quarrel among theologians, but a necessary battle for the church's preservation. Hermann Sasse, "Church and Lord's Supper," *The Lonely Way*, vol. 1, p. 419.

2. Come together man by man, in common, through grace, individually, in one faith . . . with an undivided mind, breaking one and the same bread, which is the medicine of immortality, and the antidote to prevent us from dying, but [which causes] that we should live forever in Jesus Christ. Ignatius of Antioch, *Letter to the Ephesians*, chap. 20.

3. For My thoughts are not your thoughts . . . declares the LORD. . . . So shall My word be that goes out from My mouth; it shall not return to Me empty, but it shall accomplish that which I purpose. (Isaiah 55:11)

---

6   Sasse, *The Lonely Way*, vol. 1, p. 388, footnote.

CHAPTER 8: WHAT DID JOHN TOUCH?

1. No obscurity in the words Jesus spoke at the institution of the Supper is therefore responsible for the deeply regrettable eucharistic controversies, but only the assumption that he could not have meant what is expressed in the Words of Institution because these words as they stand assert something *impossible*. Hermann Sasse, "Church and Lord's Supper," *The Lonely Way*, vol. 1, p. 405.

2. Therefore, in order that we may become of His Body, not in desire only, but also in very fact, let us become commingled with that Body. This, in truth, takes place by means of the food which He has given us as a gift, because He desired to prove the love which He has for us. It is for this reason that He has shared Himself with us and brought His body down to our level, namely, that, we might be one with Him as the body is joined with the Head. . . . And to show the love He has for us He has made it possible for those who desire, not merely to look upon Him, but even to touch Him and consume Him . . . in short to fulfill their love. John Chrysostom, *Homily 46 on the Gospel of John*, 3.

3. And the angel of the LORD appeared to him in a flame of fire out of the midst of a bush. He looked, and behold, the bush was burning, yet it was not consumed. (Exodus 3:2)

CHAPTER 9: WHAT (ON EARTH!) IS JESUS DOING?

1. The only thing that might be construed as missing from the Words of Institution would be an explanation of *how it is possible* for the bread he held in his hands to be his body. . . . Yet Jesus did not offer such an explanation on the occasion of any of his miracles. Hermann Sasse, "Church and Lord's Supper," *The Lonely Way*, vol. 1, p. 404.

2. Manifoldly does Christ initiate us by these words, and since His Discourse is hard of attainment by the more unlearned, asking for itself rather the understanding of faith than investigation. Cyril of Alexandria, *On John*, Book 4, 2, 56.

3. Do you know when the mountain goats give birth? . . . Is it by your understanding that the hawk soars . . . ? Shall a faultfinder contend with the Almighty? . . . Will you condemn Me that you may be in the right? (Job 39:1, 26; 40:2, 8)

CONCLUSION

1. Patience is one of the things that distinguishes the Church from the sect. The sect must have everything at once. It cannot wait, because it has no future. The Church can wait, because it has a future. Hermann Sasse, "Sermon for Advent I," November 29, 1936.

2. You are fond of contention, brothers, and full of zeal about things which do not pertain to salvation. Look carefully to the Scriptures, which are the true utterances of the Holy Spirit. 1 Clement 45.

3. I am with you always. (Matthew 28:20)

THE POETRY OF FAITH ALONE

1. Ignatius of Antioch, *The Epistle to the Ephesians*, 20:2.

2. Thomas Aquinas, *Catechism of the Catholic Church*, 1991, S1381.

3. Dr. Hermann Sasse, "Church and Lord's Supper," *The Lonely Way*, vol. 1, p. 419.

4. Dr. Hermann Sasse, "Church and Lord's Supper," *The Lonely Way*, vol. 1, p. 397.

More Quotes from the Fathers for Consideration

THE FOLLOWING are quotes I found in the course of preparing this work. There are definitely many more among the ancient fathers, but these are what I was led to. Along with some of Calvin's most direct statements against the Supper, they are all left here for your consideration and, perhaps, devotion.

THE DIDACHE OF THE APOSTLES

But every Lord's day gather yourselves together, and break bread. (14)

THE APOSTLES' CREED

I believe in the communion of the saints.

THE APOLOGETICS OF IRENAEUS

For as the bread, which is produced from the earth, when it receives the invocation of God, is no longer common bread, but the Eucharist, consisting of two realities, earthly and heavenly; so also our bodies, when they receive the Eucharist, are no longer corruptible, having the hope of the resurrection. *Against Heresies*, IV.18.5.

JUSTIN, THE MARTYR

And this food is called among us [Εὐχαριστία] the Eucharist, of which no one is allowed to partake but the man who believes that the things which we teach are true, and who has been washed with the washing that is for the remission of sins, and unto regeneration, and who is so living as Christ has enjoined. For not as common bread and common drink do we receive these; but in like manner as Jesus Christ our Saviour, having been made flesh by the Word of God, had both flesh and blood for our salvation, so likewise have we been taught that the food which is blessed by the prayer of His word, and from which our blood and flesh by transmutation are nourished, is the flesh and blood of that Jesus who was made flesh. *The First and Second Apologies*, 66.[7]

THE CONFESSION OF AUGUSTINE OF HIPPO

The question is, "Where is the Church?" What, therefore, are we to do? Are we to seek it in our own words or in the words of its Head, our Lord Jesus Christ? I think that we ought to seek it in the words of Him who is Truth, and who knows His own body best. *Against the Donatists*, IV, 15:2.

THE LITURGICAL FORMULAE OF THE APOSTOLIC CONSTITUTIONS

[The pastor holds up the consecrated bread and says,] *The consecrated things for the consecrated people.*

[The congregation responds,] *There is One that is consecrated; there is one Lord, one Jesus Christ, blessed forever, to the glory of the Father. Amen.* (13)

THE WITNESS OF CYRIL OF ALEXANDRIA

SINCE THE flesh of the Saviour hath become life-giving (as being united to that which is by nature Life, the Word from God), when we taste it, then have we life in ourselves. . . .

Since Christ is in us through his own flesh, we shall surely rise. For it were incredible, yea rather impossible, that Life should not make alive

---

7   Also found in Sasse, *The Lonely Way*, vol. 1, p. 379, footnote.

those in whom it is. For as if one took a spark and buried it amid much stubble, in order that the seed of fire preserved might lay hold on it, so in us too our Lord Jesus Christ hideth life through his own flesh, and inserts it as a seed of immortality, abolishing the whole corruption that is in us.

Manifoldly does Christ initiate us by these words, . . . asking for itself rather the understanding of faith than investigation. . . . For "he that eateth My flesh" (saith He) "and drinketh My blood abideth in Me and I in him." . . . He who receiveth "the flesh" of our Saviour Christ and "drinketh His" precious "blood," as He saith, is found one with Him, commingled as it were and immingled with Him through the participation, so that he is found in Christ, Christ again in him. *On John*, Book 4, 2, 53–55.

We do not deny that we are joined to Christ spiritually by true faith and sincere love. But we do deny that we have no kind of connection with him according to the flesh, and we say that this would be completely foreign to the sacred Scriptures. Who has ever doubted that Christ is a vine in this way and that we are truly branches, deriving life from him for ourselves? Listen to Paul say, "We are all one Body in Christ," . . . "We who are many are one body, for we all partake of the same loaf." . . . Does he think perhaps that we do not know the power of the mystical benediction? Since this is in us, does it not also cause Christ to dwell in us bodily through the communication of the flesh of Christ? . . . Therefore, we must consider that Christ is in us, not only according to the habit which we understand as love, but also by a natural participation." On John 10:2, from Tappert, *The Book of Concord*, 179.

THE DYING WORDS OF THOMAS AQUINAS

If in this world there be any knowledge of this Sacrament stronger than faith, I wish now to use it in affirming that I firmly believe and know as certain that Jesus Christ, true God and true Man, Son of God and Son of the Virgin Mary, is in this Sacrament. I receive thee the price of my redemption, for whose love I have watched, studied, and labored. Thee have I preached; thee have I taught. *The Catholic Encyclopedia*, entry on Thomas Aquinas.

THE PEN OF DR. MARTIN LUTHER

How can bodily eating and drinking do such great things? Certainly not just eating and drinking do these things, but the words written here: "Given and shed for you for the forgiveness of sins." These words, along with the bodily eating and drinking, are the main thing in the Sacrament. Whoever believes these words has exactly what they say: "forgiveness of sins." Luther's Small Catechism, "The Sacrament of the Altar."

The heart cannot eat it physically and the body cannot eat it spiritually. Luther's Works, WA:23.191–19–20.

I believe and do not doubt, and shall also with the help and grace of my dear Lord Jesus Christ adhere to this confession until the last day, that where mass is celebrated according to Christ's ordinance, be it among us Lutherans or under the papacy or in Greece or in India . . . nevertheless, under the form of bread, the true body of Christ, given for us on the cross, under the form of wine, the true blood of Christ, shed for us, are present; furthermore, it is not a spiritual or imagined body and blood but the genuine natural body and blood derived from the holy, virginal, true, human body of Mary, conceived without a human body by the Holy Spirit alone. This body and blood of Christ are even now sitting at the right hand of God in majesty, in the divine person called Jesus Christ, who is genuine, true, eternal God with the Father of whom he was born from eternity, etc. This body and this blood of the Son of God, Jesus Christ, not only the holy and worthy but also sinners and the unworthy truly administer and receive bodily, although invisibly, with their hands, their mouths, the chalice, paten, corporal, and what they use for this purpose when it is administered and received in the mass.

This is my faith; this I know, and no one shall wrest it from me. Luther's Works, WA 38.264.26. ff. (The English translation is from *LW* [AE] 38:224.)[8]

Since I see that as time wears on, sects and errors increase, and that there is no end to the rage and fury of Satan, in order that henceforth during my life or after my death some of them may not, in future, support themselves by me, and falsely quote my writings to strengthen their error as the Sacramentarians and Anabaptists begin to do, I mean by this writing to confess my faith, point by point [concerning all the articles of

---

8   Sasse, *The Lonely Way*, vol. 1, p. 387.

our religion], before God and all the world, in which I intend to abide until my death, and therein (so help me God!) to depart from this world and to appear before the judgment-seat of Jesus Christ.

And if after my death any one should say: If Dr. Luther were living now, he would teach and hold this or that article differently, for he did not sufficiently consider it, against this I say now as then, and then as now, that, by God's grace, I have most diligently, compared all these articles with the Scriptures time and again [have examined them, not once, but very often, according to the standard of Holy Scripture], and often have gone over them, and would defend them as confidently as I have now defended the Sacrament of the Altar.

I am not drunk nor thoughtless; I know what I say; I also am sensible of what it means for me at the coming of the Lord Christ at the final judgment. Therefore I want no one to regard this as a jest or mere idle talk; it is a serious matter to me; for by God's grace I know Satan a good deal; if he can pervert or confuse God's Word, what will he not do with my words or those of another? Solid Declaration of the Formula of Concord, Article VII, 29–31.

THE SKEPTICISM OF CALVIN

But, I ask, what did Christ give to his disciples the day before he suffered? Do not the words say that he gave the mortal body, which was to be delivered shortly after? John Calvin, *Institutes of the Christian Religion*, book 4, chap. 17, 17.

Were this rule admitted, complete barbarism would bury the whole light of faith. What monstrous absurdities shall fanatical men not be able to extract, if they are allowed to urge every knotty point [of Scripture] in support of their dogmas? Calvin, *Institutes of the Christian Religion*, book 4, chap. 17, 23.

I have no doubt that he will truly give and I receive. Only, I reject the absurdities which appear to be unworthy of the heavenly majesty of Christ, and are inconsistent with the reality of his human nature. . . . Because it is enough for us, that Christ, out of the substance of his flesh, breathes life into our souls, nay, diffuses his own life into us, though the real flesh of Christ does not enter us. Calvin, *Institutes of the Christian Religion*, book 4, chap. 17, 32.

Though philosophically speaking, there is no "place" above the heavens, nevertheless, because the body of Christ, as the nature and mode of a human body calls for, is finite and is contained in heaven, as in a place, it is necessary that it be distant from us by so great an interval of space as heaven is removed from the earth. . . . For since the signs are here on earth, are observed with the eyes, softly touched by the hands, Christ, as far as He is man, is to be sought nowhere else than in heaven and not otherwise than with the mind and the intelligence of faith. (*Consensus Tirgunus*, 25). Hermann Sasse, "Church and Lord's Supper," *The Lonely Way*, vol. 1, pp. 427–28, footnote.

A note from Sasse on reading Calvin's essential arguments:

[Calvin's] explanation of the Supper texts is determined by the preconception that Christ's body cannot enter into us. For Calvin, the body of Christ as a truly human body exists in finite form and must, therefore, after the exaltation be as far removed from us as heaven is from earth. . . . Calvin is not in a position to substantiate these assertions from the Bible, for he did not derive them from the Bible. These are metaphysical statements and ideological presuppositions that he uses to explain the Supper texts. Hermann Sasse, "Church and Lord's Supper," *The Lonely Way*, vol. 1, p. 414.

THE BOLDNESS OF NICHOLAS SELNECKER

When our churches use the ancient little words "the body of Christ is taken in the bread . . ." they do not postulate thereby any "inclusion" or "consubstantiation" or "putting together," but nothing more or less is meant than . . . that Christ is truthful and that when he gives us the bread in the Supper, he at the same time gives us his body to eat, as he himself expresses it.

So if we retain only the Lord's body in the Supper, it makes no difference to us whether people say "in the bread" or "with the bread" or "under the bread" or even omit these little words entirely. We will not let the body of Christ be taken from us even at the price of our body and life, honor, property and blood. And we appeal herewith to the countenance, throne and judgment of Christ, and we cite and invite thither all who counter his express testament and institution by dreaming up an absent body in the Supper or propounding a figurative interpretation. *Concerning the Supper of the Lord*, E2.

THE CRASS UNBELIEF OF WILHELM HEITMÜLLER

When Jesus in that solemn hour distributed his body . . . he meant himself, his personality, what his personality determined and guaranteed by way of religious substance and experience: he meant a purely personal, spiritual, and ethical communion. . . . [But] naturalistic, mystical elements usurped this communion with Jesus, the idea of spiritual and bodily union with the exalted one forced its way in, and, in connection with this, there crept in, from the undercurrent of popular religion, a belief in the mediation of spiritual goods by external actions and "material" means. The holy meal became supernatural food, bread and cup mediated Christ's body and blood: sacramental belief made its entrance. The first beginnings of this fateful development manifest themselves already in Paul. Hermann Sasse, *The Lonely Way*, vol. 1, pp. 415–16.

It is certain that this understanding is very ancient, that it was already present in ancient Christendom at least in a similar form in Paul, and that the writers and first readers of the Gospels understood the words in a similar way. We sincerely admire the deep mysticism and believing ardor that have in all ages found contentment and experienced their culmination in this eucharistic faith. But none of this justifies the view that Jesus himself intended these words this way. Hermann Sasse, *The Lonely Way*, vol. 1, pp. 417–18.

(Notice how from the fine modernist perspective of eighteen hundred years later, he accuses the churches of mythologizing Jesus' meaning, but he must also lay the blame at the very words of Paul and the Gospel writers for making this "mistake"!)

THE STEADFASTNESS OF HERMANN SASSE

Whether the ancient world waxed indignant over alleged cannibalism on the part of Christians or the modern world turns up its nose with Frederick the Great, [saying] "that they eat their God," for both the wise and the fools of this world, the Supper remains in equal measure incomprehensible and insupportable—at the very least an insult to human reason. So it always has been and so it will always remain. *The Lonely Way*, vol. 1, p. 419.

No obscurity in the words Jesus spoke at the institution of the Supper is therefore responsible for the deeply regrettable eucharistic controversies, but only the assumption that he could not have meant what is expressed in the Words of Institution because these words as they stand assert something *impossible*. *The Lonely Way*, vol. 1, p. 405.

The Supper keeps the church from becoming a church without hope. *The Lonely Way*, vol. 1, p. 422.

In the Supper, time touches eternity and the here and now meets the beyond. It is the meal of pilgrims, *cibus viatorum* ["food of travelers"] as our medieval fathers used to call it. It is eaten on the migration from the world to the kingdom of God, from time to eternity, from the here and now to the beyond. *The Lonely Way*, vol. 1, p. 393.

The Sacrament can be rightly administered only where the Gospel is purely taught, and the proclamation of the Gospel can remain pure only where Christ's Sacrament is rightly celebrated. *The Lonely Way*, vol. 1, p. 429.

Word and Sacrament, Gospel and Lord's Supper belong indissolubly together. . . . [Christ] builds his church . . . neither through the Word alone, nor through the Sacrament alone, but through both together. *The Lonely Way*, vol. 1, p. 429.

The fate of a church that has lost the Sacrament of the Altar is clear. A church that does not continually gather around the Supper must undergo *secularization*. It must irreversibly turn into a piece of the world, because the Supper establishes the boundary between church and world. This conclusion is confirmed by the experience of church history and especially of the history of worship in the last few centuries. The destruction of the Supper is followed by the disappearance of the living *remembrance* of Jesus from the hearts of Christians, especially his suffering and death. *The Lonely Way*, vol. 1, p. 420.

Christ can be forgotten in preaching, but he cannot be forgotten in the Supper. *The Lonely Way*, vol. 1, p. 383.

EVERYWHERE that the Supper's needfulness with respect to the essence of the Church was no longer understood, wherever people were allowed to think of the Church as existing apart from the Supper, wherever the Supper was retained merely out of obedience or piety but not out of a deep longing for the unique gift of this Sacrament—in all these places the Supper itself died with the hunger and thirst for the Sacrament, and the Church died with the Supper.

If the celebration of the Supper should cease, then the preaching of the Word would be struck dumb, with the result that faith would be quenched, love would grow cold, and hope would die. Where the heart dies, the body dies also. *The Church dies with the Supper. The Lonely Way*, vol. 1, p. 425.

Christ's sacrifice turns from reality into an idea, and the vicarious satisfaction for sins turns from a fact into a theory. . . . The doctrine will then very soon turn into a topic for general philosophical discussion. . . . Where the church no longer proclaims the Lord's death at the altar "until he comes," the maranatha falls silent. . . . In the long run they cannot endure the disappointment involved in the delay of the parousia. . . . For this reason a symbolic, spiritualistic doctrine of the Supper has, as a rule, resulted in a symbolic, spiritualistic doctrine of the last things. This becomes especially clear in the matter of *belief in the resurrection. The Lonely Way*, vol. 1, p. 421.

"That Rock was Christ." . . . Even though it strikes the contemporary exegete with his modern scholarly methods as strange, and while it could never be achieved by our human means, this unquestionably correct interpretation of the OT by an apostle of Christ is a genuine aid to our understanding. *The Lonely Way,* vol. 1, pp. 410–11.

We absolutely do not understand why this paradox should be thought any greater than those involved in the doctrine of the two natures of Christ or the doctrine of the Trinity. *The Lonely Way*, vol. 1, p. 406.

The soul cannot eat and the body cannot believe. *The Lonely Way*, vol. 1, p. 423.

How often have people imagined themselves to be gathered in Jesus' name, when in fact they were only gathered in their own! How often have they believed themselves able to subject the presence of Christ to sense perception . . . when in fact they have merely imagined this presence! How often have people believed themselves to have experienced the communion of saints when what they experienced was not the communion of the Holy Spirit but just a communion of the pious flesh! Hymns . . . have never been sung with greater ardor than in the worst sects known to church history. *The Lonely Way*, vol. 1, p. 398.

Today there are perhaps entire countries in which, notwithstanding the sacrifice of the Mass, the Roman Sacrament of the Altar has preserved more remnants of the biblical Lord's Supper than has what the Protestants celebrate—or no longer celebrate—as the Supper. *The Lonely Way*, vol. 1, p. 418.

In times past and present, her struggle does not aim at securing a "Lutheran" Supper, but a biblical Lord's Supper, and therefore the *biblical* church and the *Christ of the Bible*. *The Lonely Way*, vol. 1, p. 429.

Scripture's teaching on the Supper is not something yet to be discovered by future synods and theological conferences, but that it has already long since been found and can be seen by everyone who reads the NT in faith in Christ, without ideological preconceptions. *The Lonely Way*, vol. 1, p. 429.

A theology that makes use of arguments of this sort [which deny the sacramental presence of Christ in the Supper in any way] bequeaths scriptural proof to the Roman Church. *The Lonely Way*, vol. 1, p. 418.

Pastors simply no longer have any clear dogmatic convictions about the Sacrament of the Altar. They content themselves with wavering subjective opinions that they choose according to personal taste and practical needs from that well-stocked warehouse of fashionable theological goods. . . . The events of recent years have already given us some inkling of the long-term consequences of this development. *The Lonely Way*, vol. 1, p. 420.

The renewal of the Christian congregation and her Divine Service [Gottesdienst, JF] therefore begins, in a way that most theologians today still find incomprehensible, when we once again seriously learn and teach what the NT and the catechism say on Baptism and the Supper. *The Lonely Way*, vol. 1, p. 395.

What is at stake for her is the supreme value for which the church can and must wage her warfare, namely, the absolute validity of the divine Word. *The Lonely Way*, vol. 1, p. 429.

THE LOSS of the dogma is the loss of Christ.

More Bible Verses

THE FOLLOWING is a list of Bible verses that, when believed within the context of the Lord's Supper, become all the more devotional:

I do not want you to be unaware, brothers. (1 Corinthians 10:1)

Therefore I intend always to remind you of these. (2 Peter 1:12)

You will be . . . trained in the words of the faith and of the good doctrine that you have followed. (1 Timothy 4:6)

If we are faithless, He remains faithful. (2 Timothy 2:13)

His body was like beryl, his face like the appearance of lightning, his eyes like flaming torches, his arms and legs like the gleam of burnished bronze. (Daniel 10:6)

He has scattered the proud in the thoughts of their hearts. (Luke 1:51)

He spoke, and it came to be. (Psalm 33:9)

I will build My church, and the gates of hell shall not prevail against it. (Matthew 16:18)

Little children, keep yourselves from idols. (1 John 5:21)

+ + +